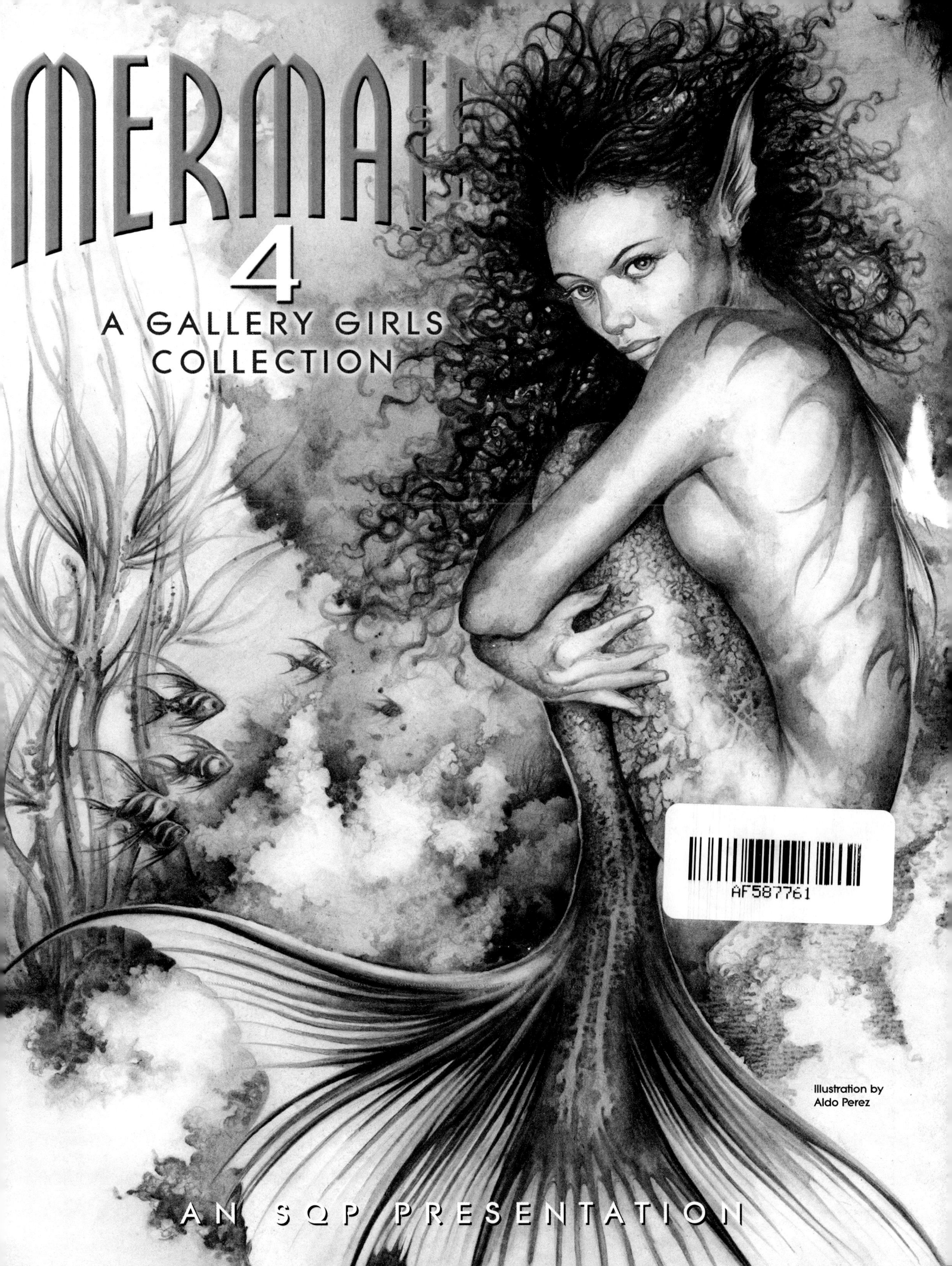
MERMAIDS
4
A GALLERY GIRLS
COLLECTION
AF587761
Illustration by
Aldo Perez
AN SQP PRESENTATION

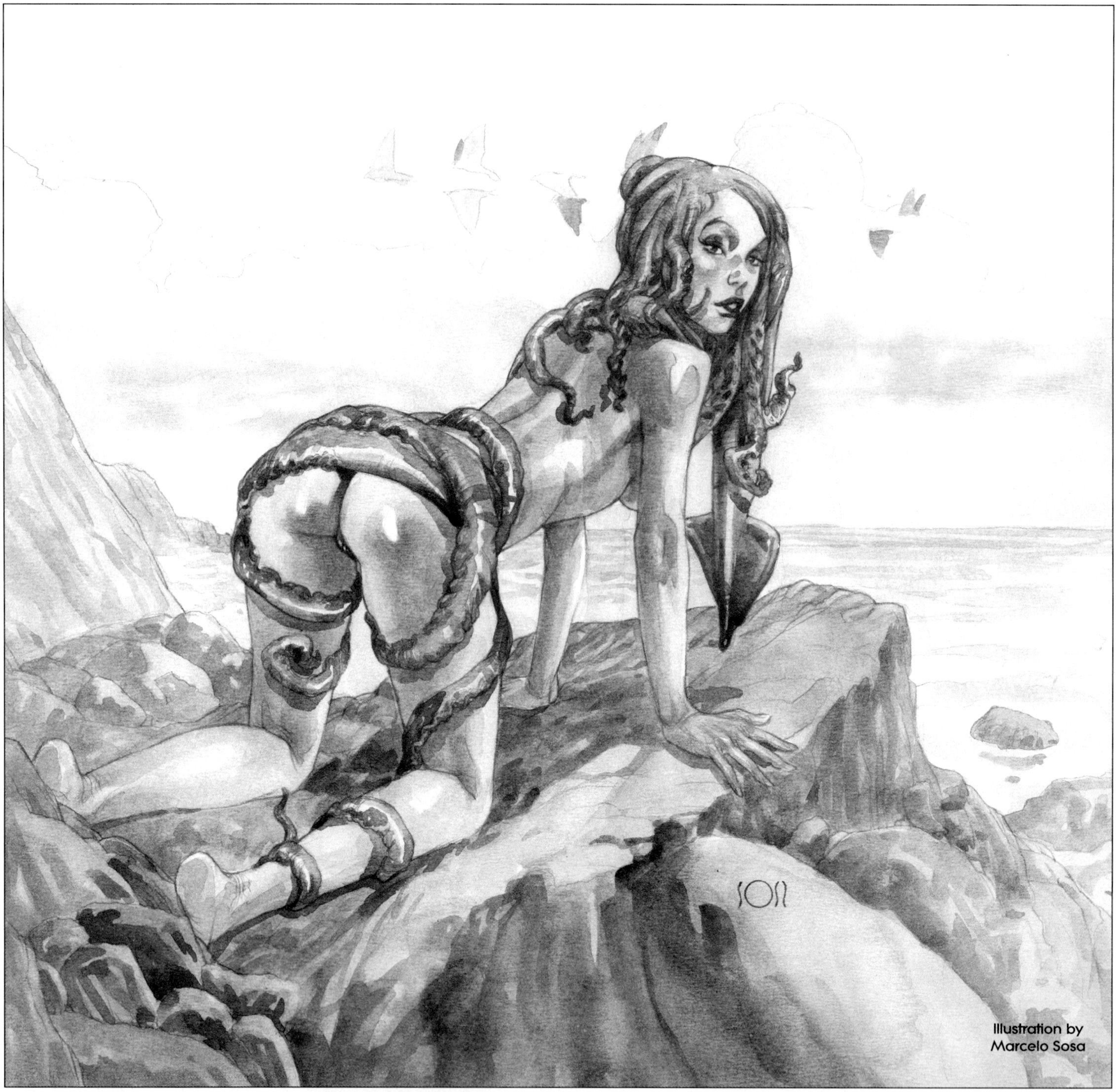

Illustration by
Marcelo Sosa

MERMAIDS

Volume Four

Book design by Grassy Knoll Studios.

Published by
SQP Inc.
PO Box 248 - Columbus, NJ 08022

Sal Quartuccio & Bob Keenan - Publishers

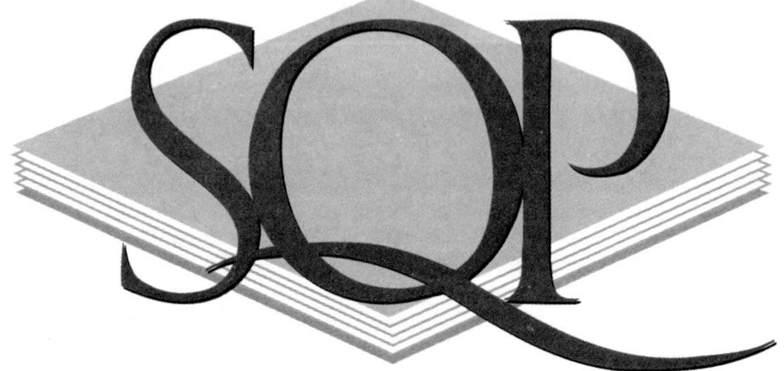

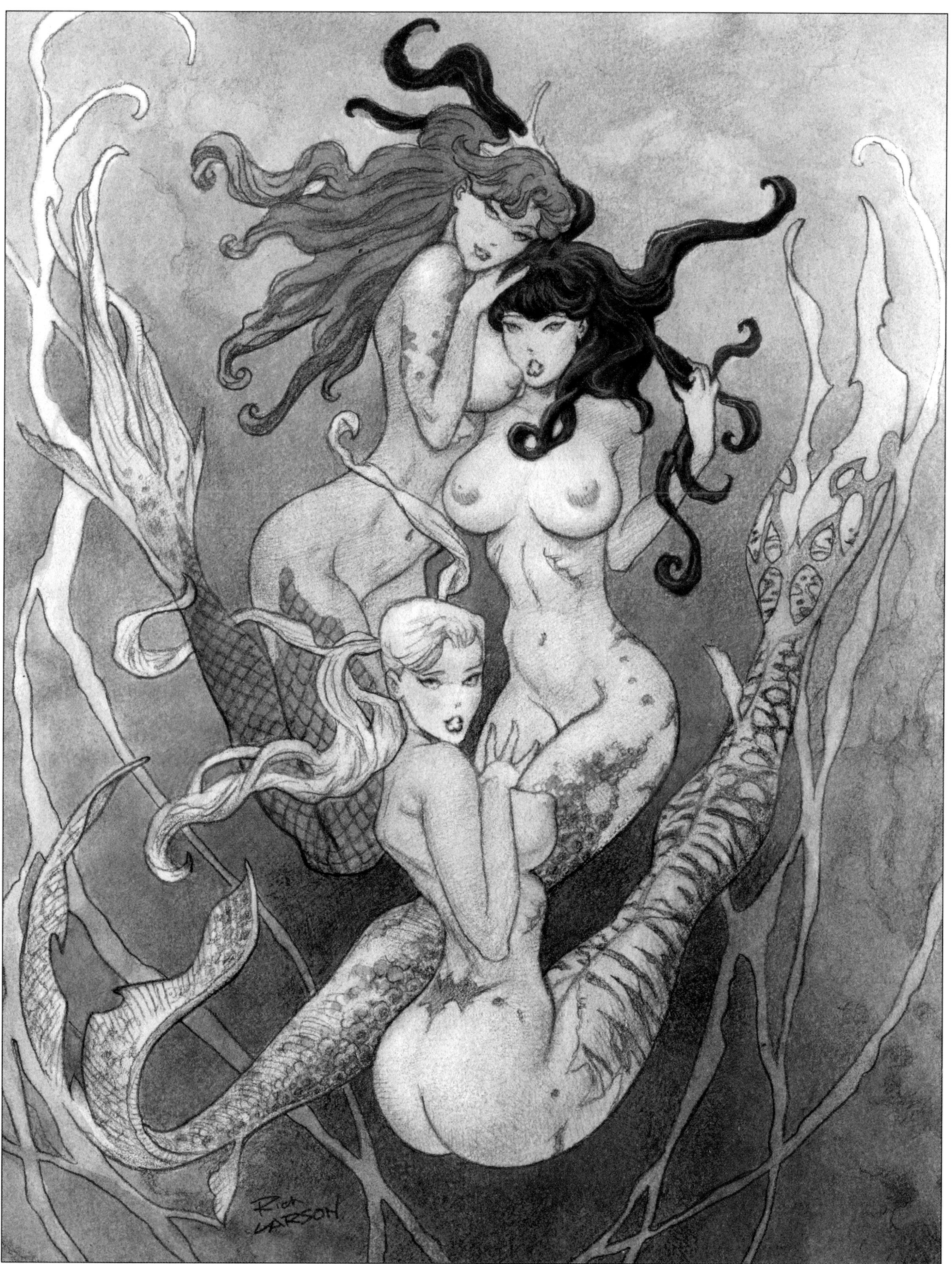

RICH LARSON

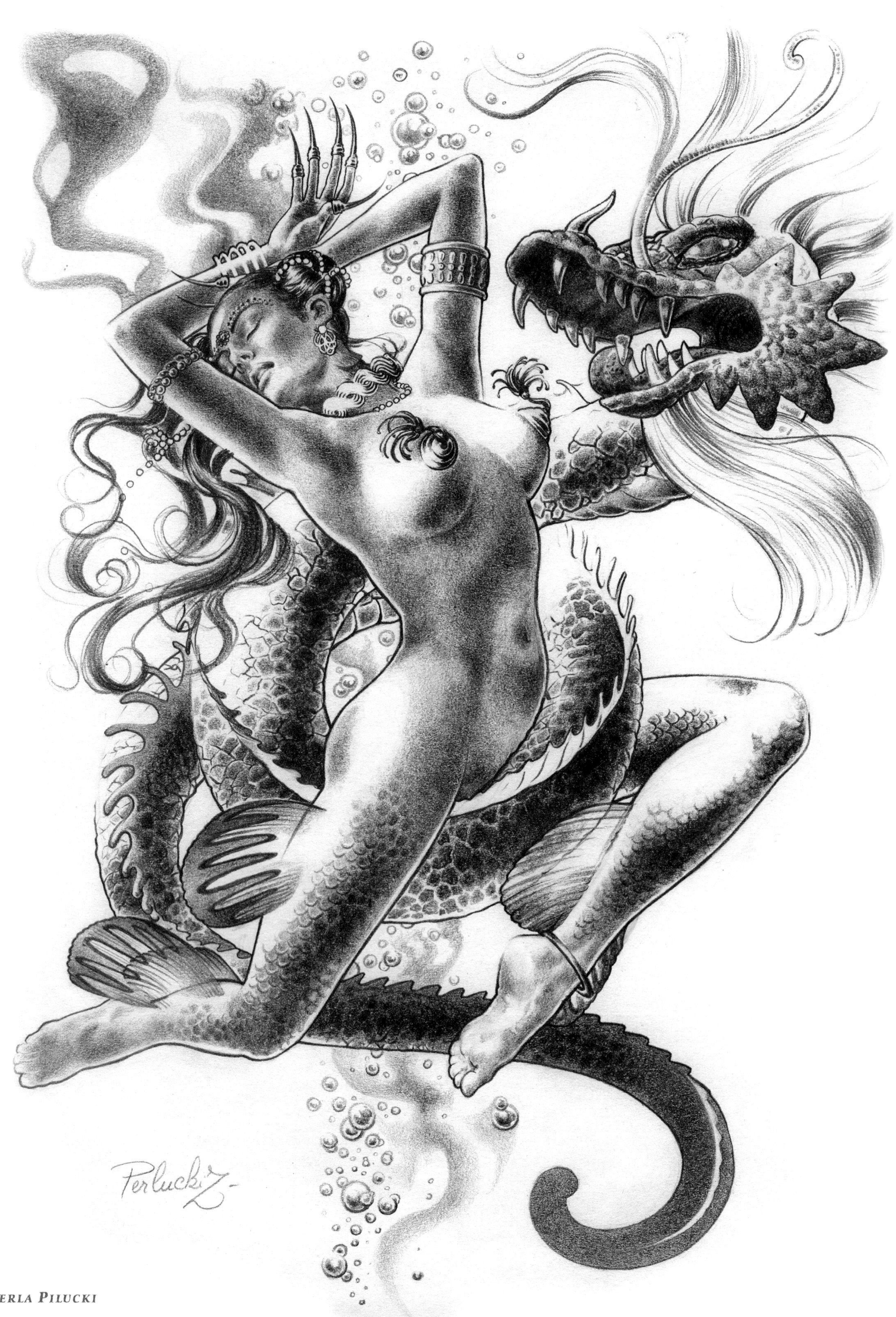

Perla Pilucki

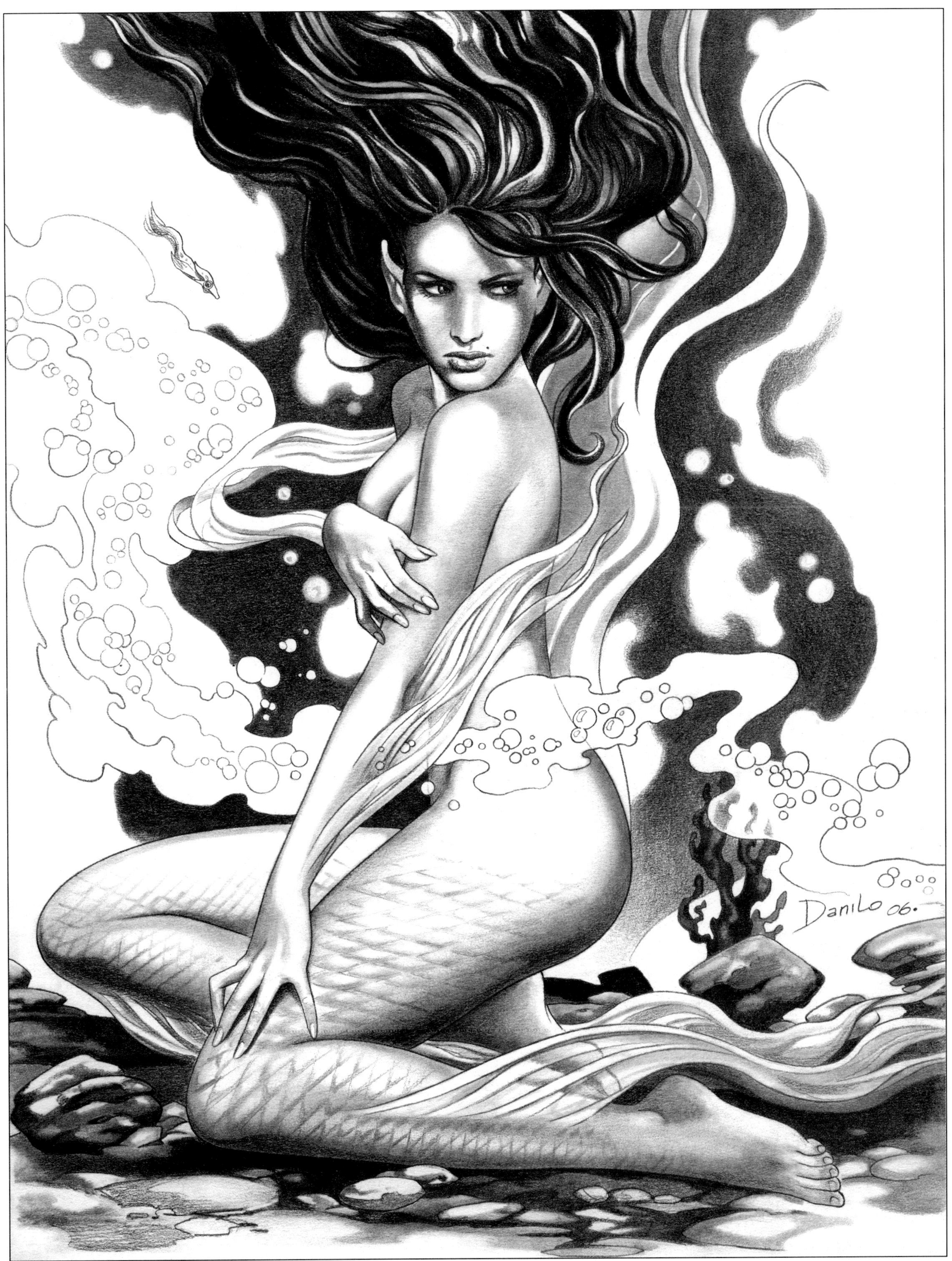

DANILO GUIDA

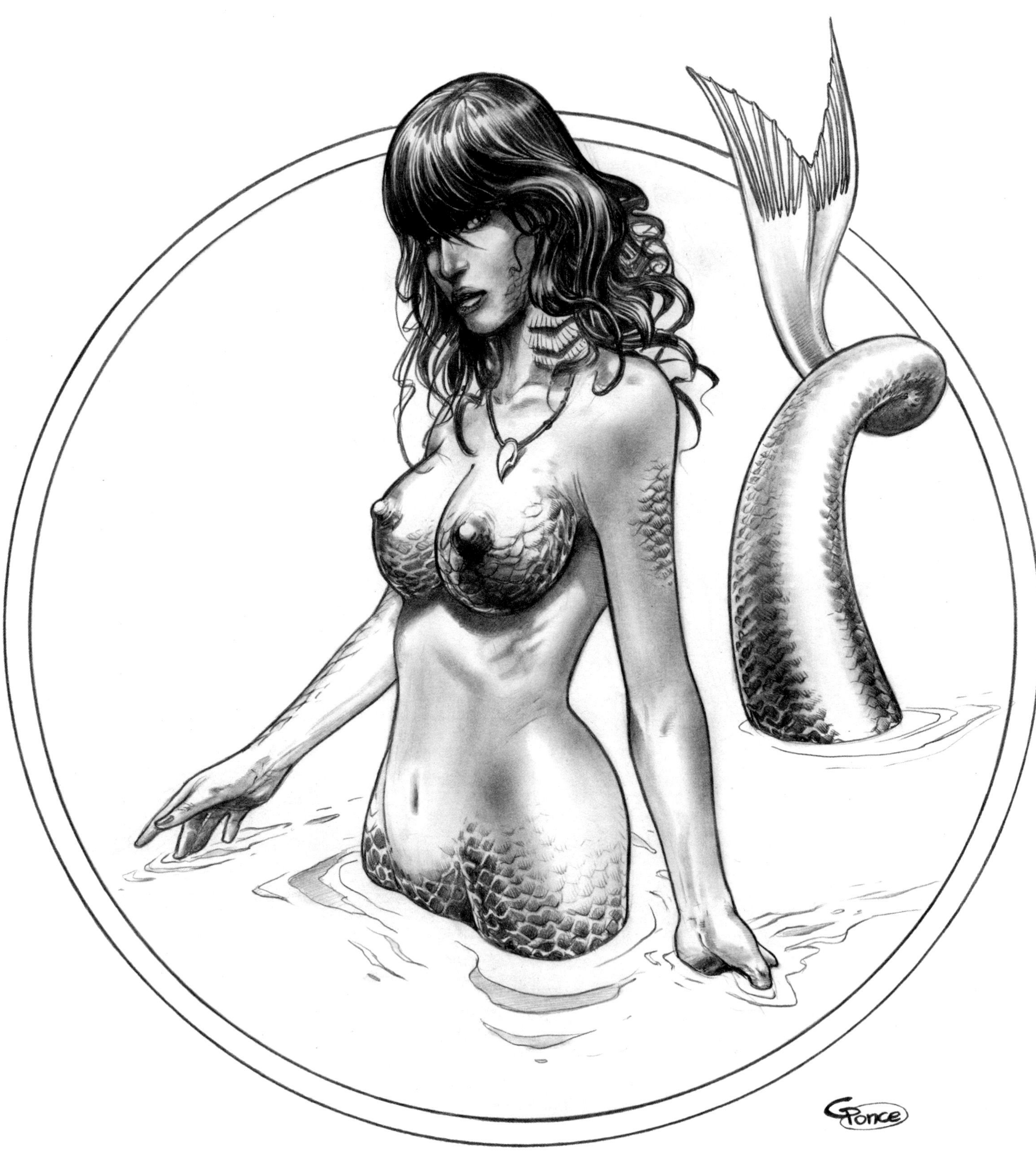

German Ponce

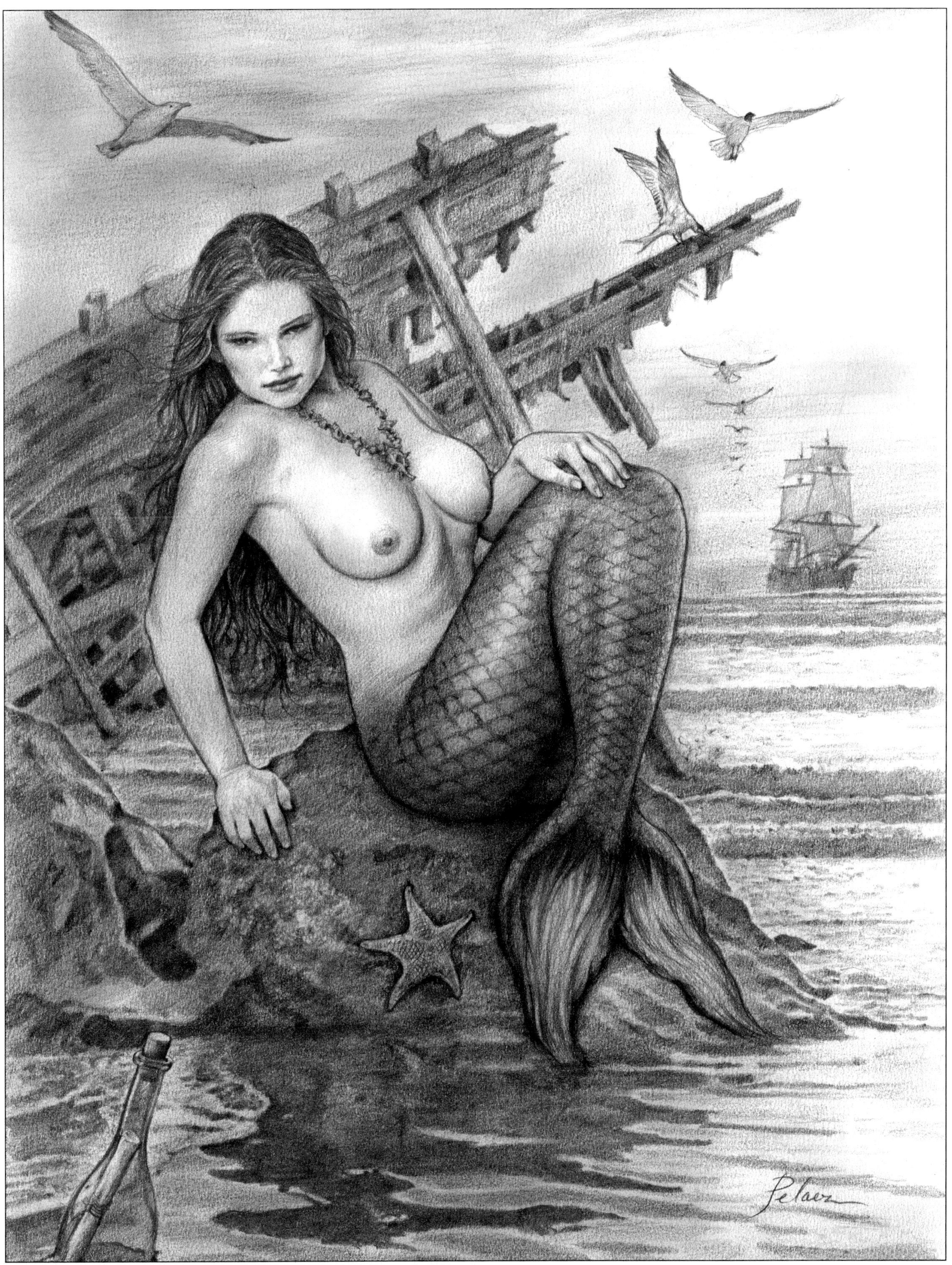

PELAEZ

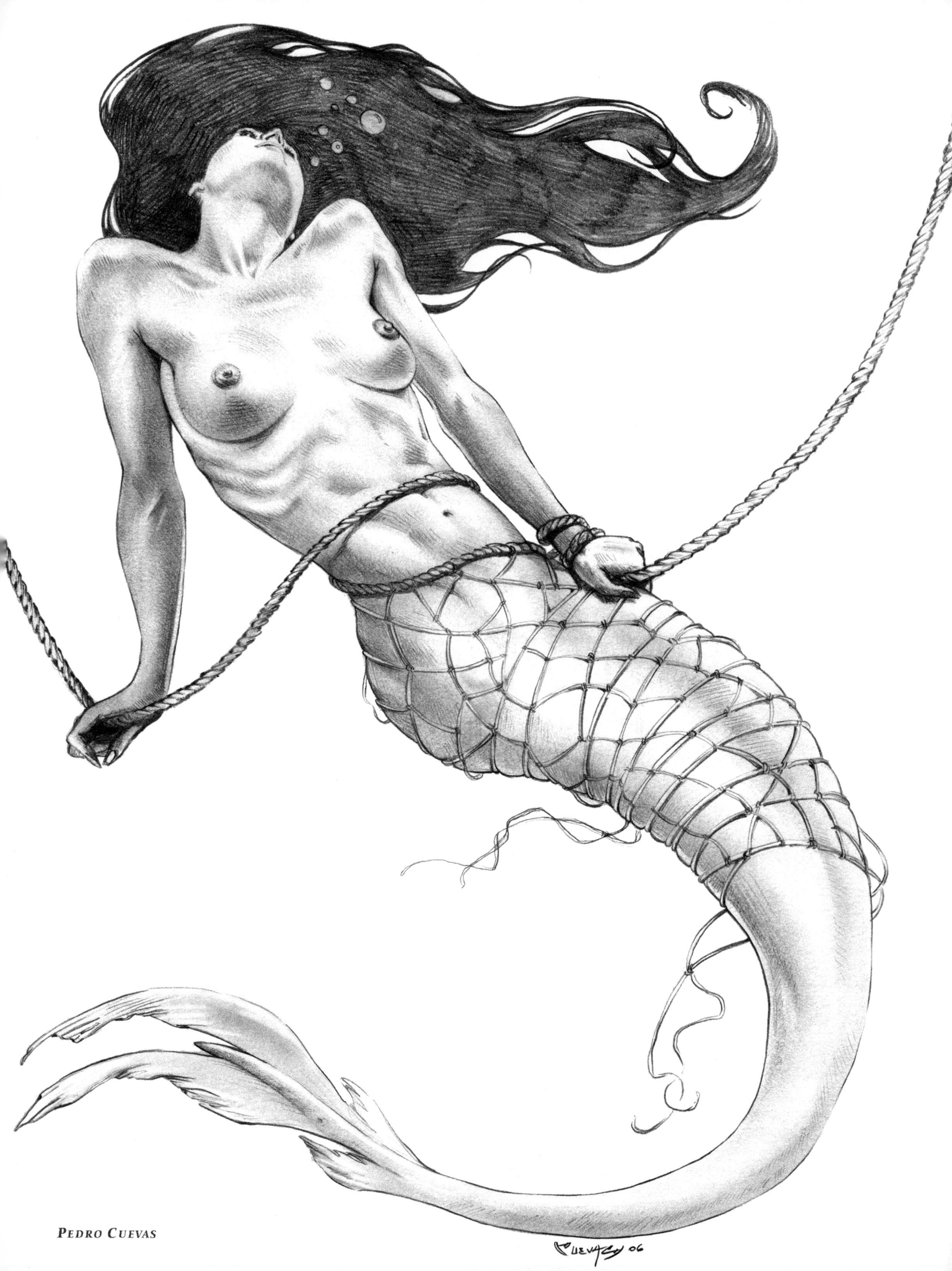

Pedro Cuevas

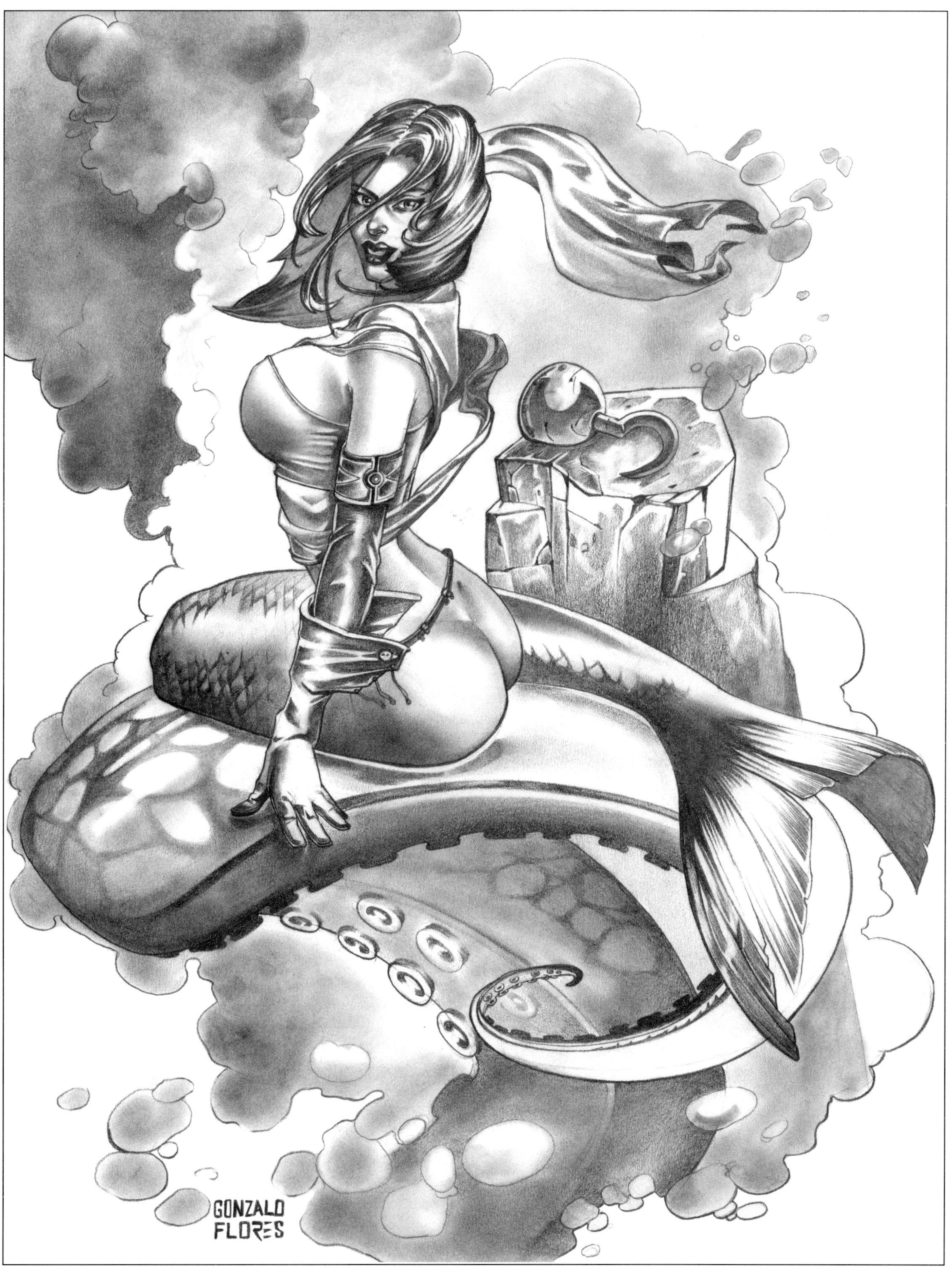

GONZALO FLORES

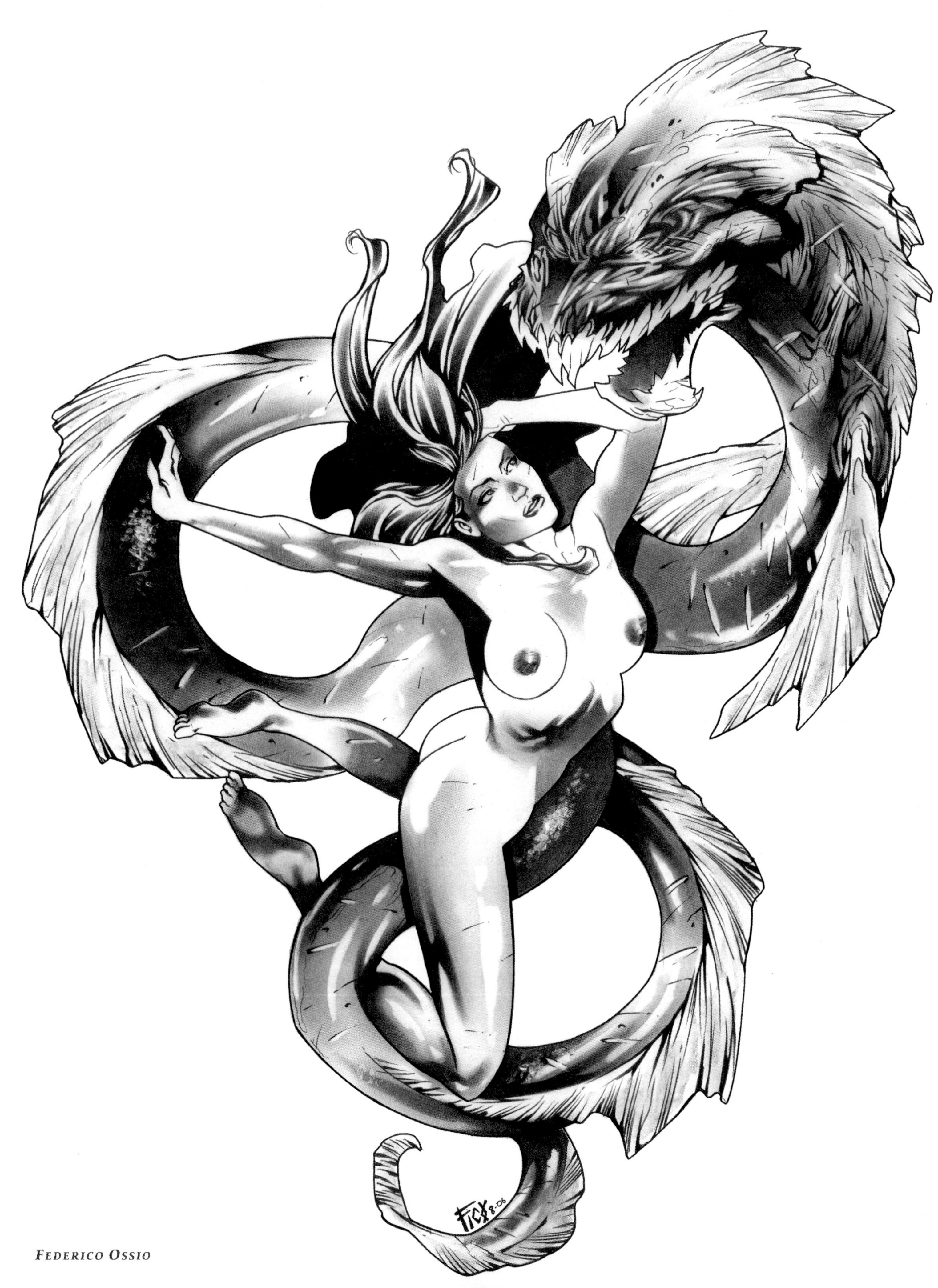

Federico Ossio

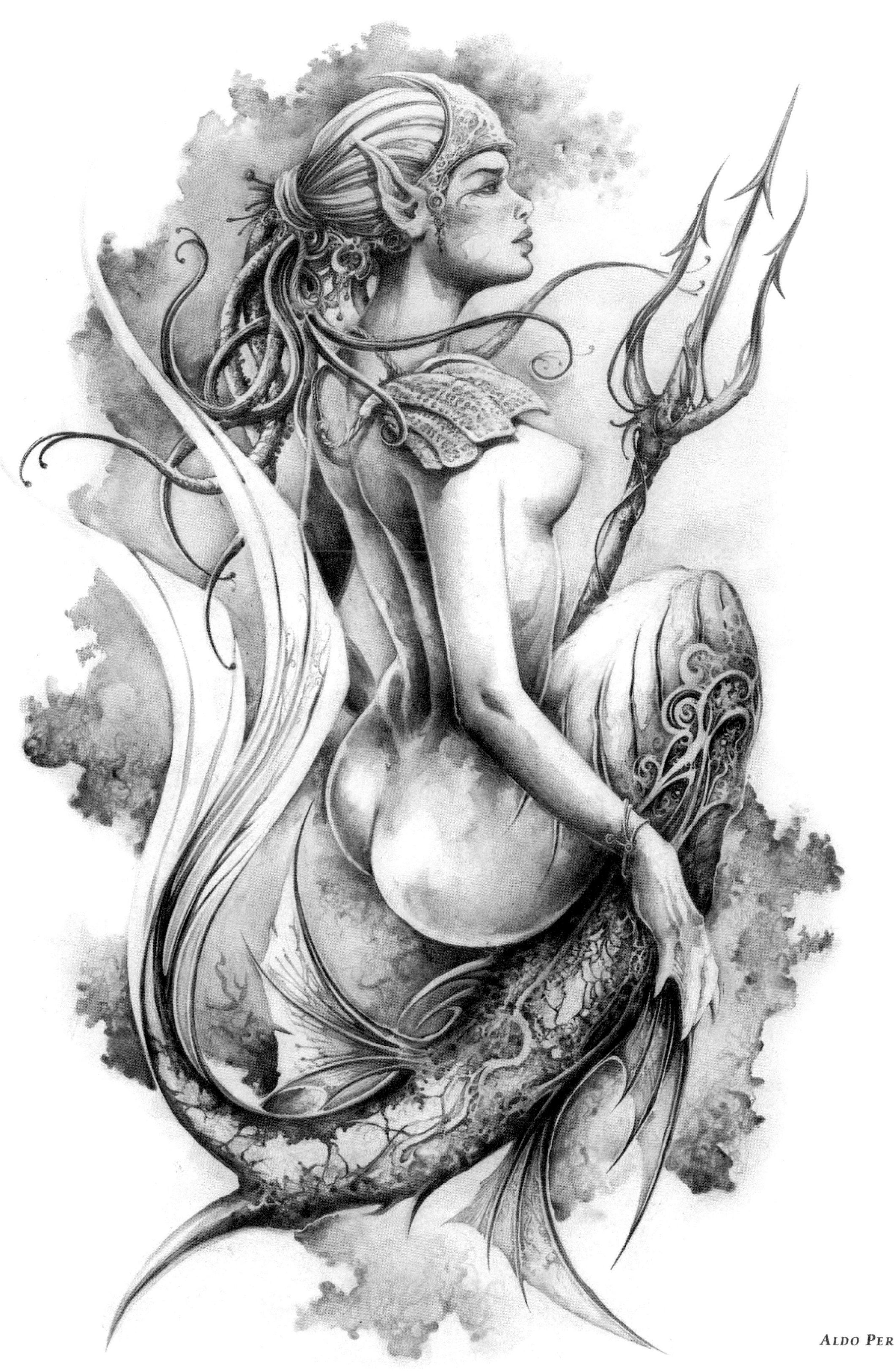

Aldo Perez

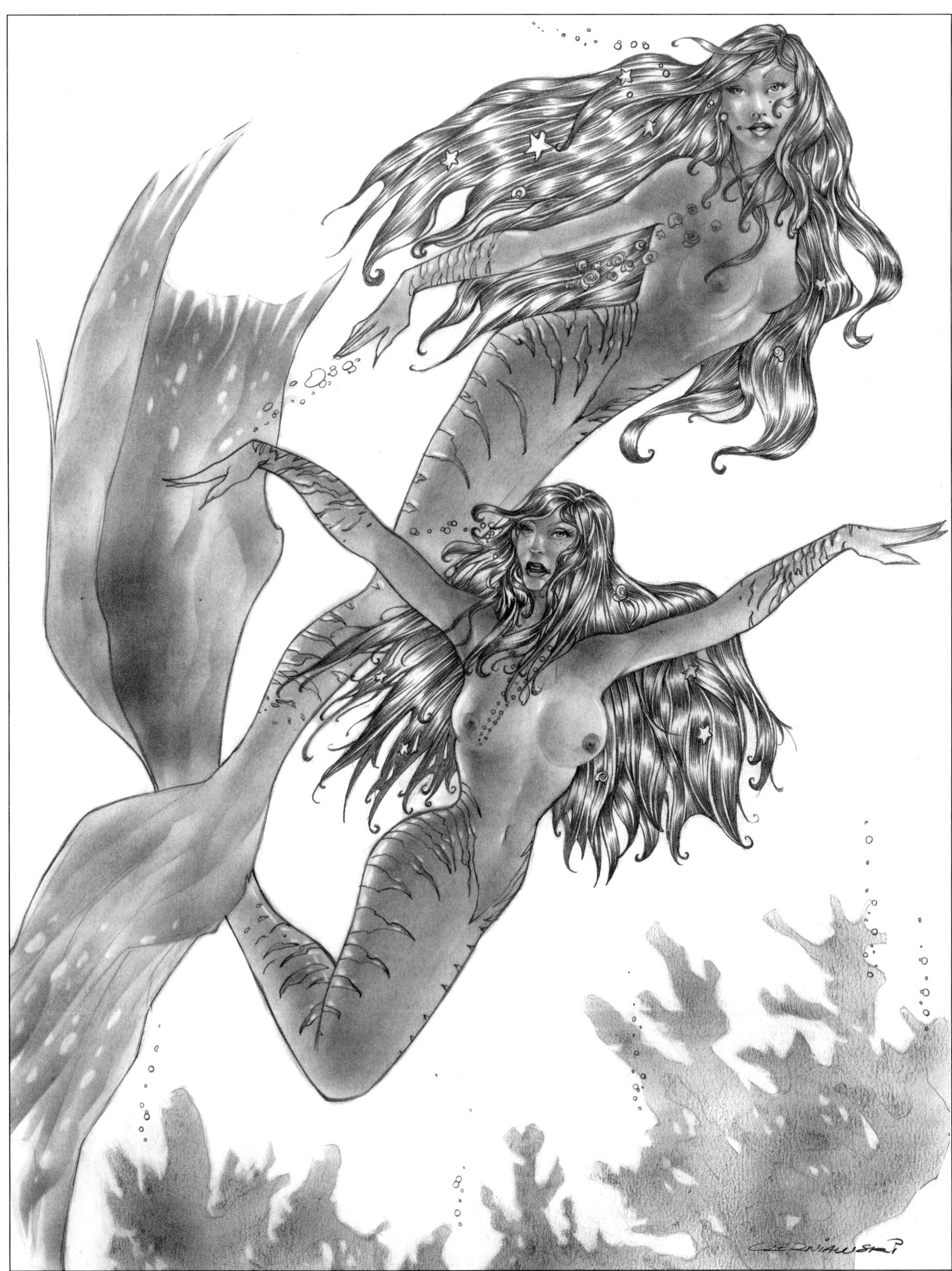

J.L. Czerniawski

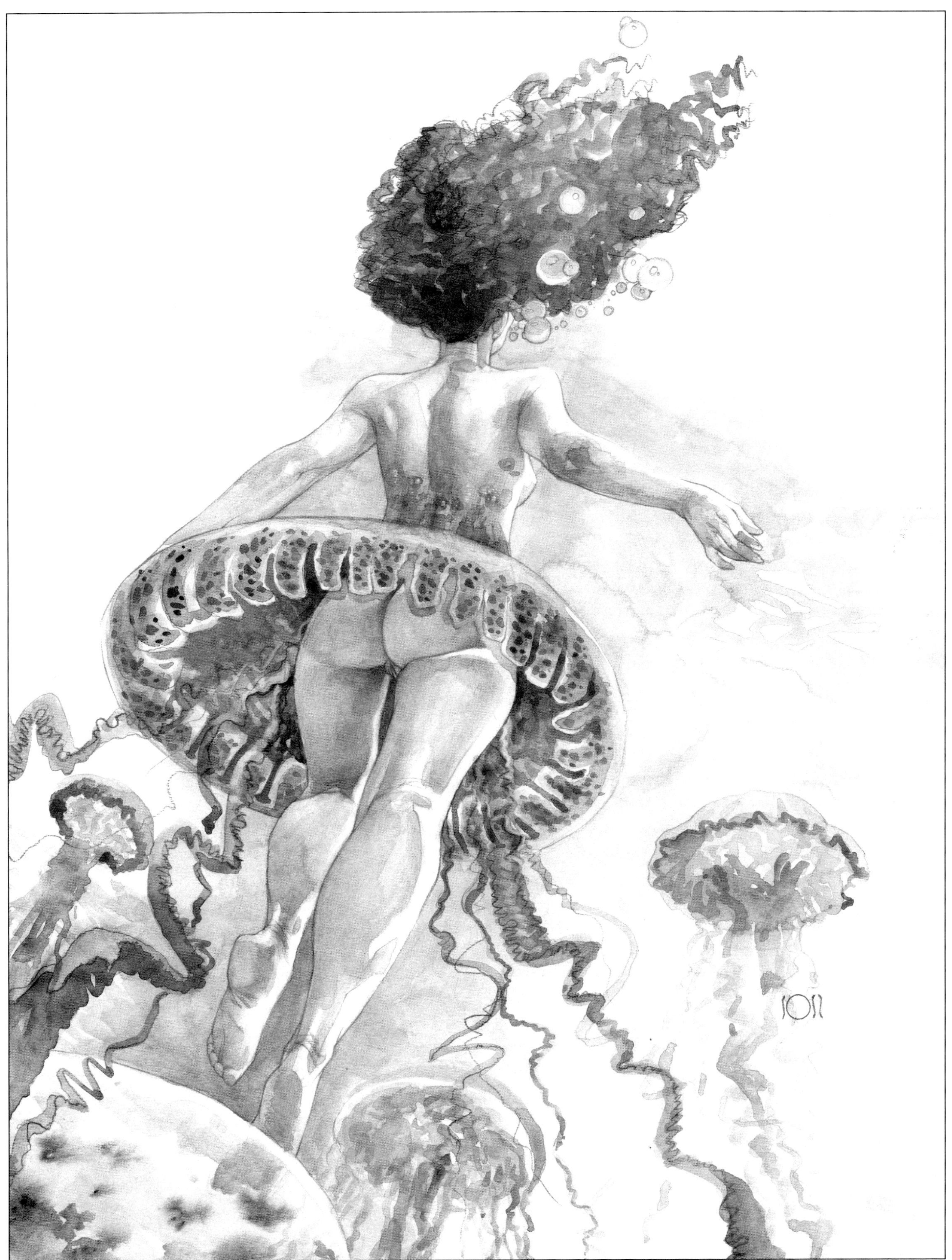

Marcelo Sosa

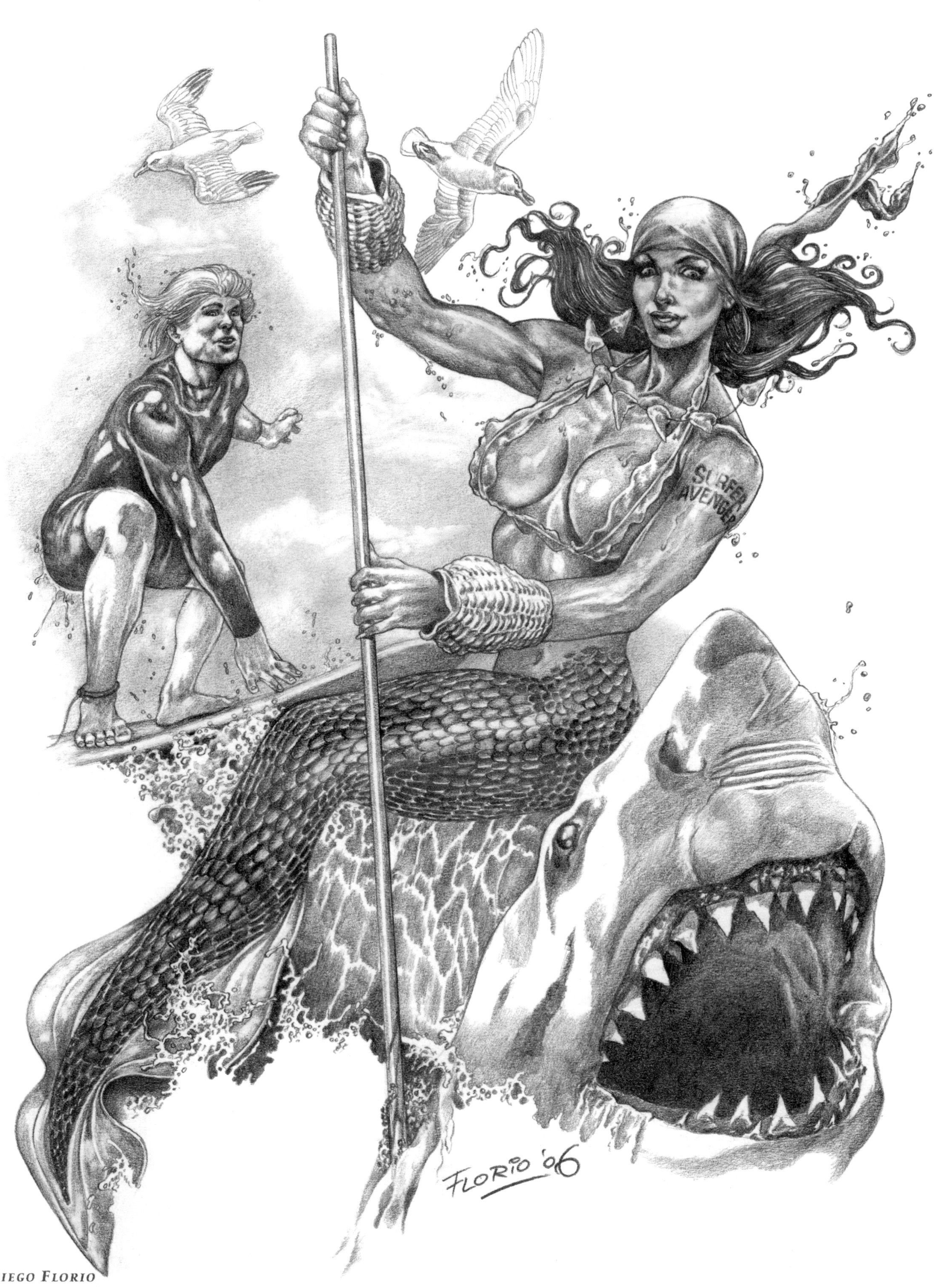

Diego Florio

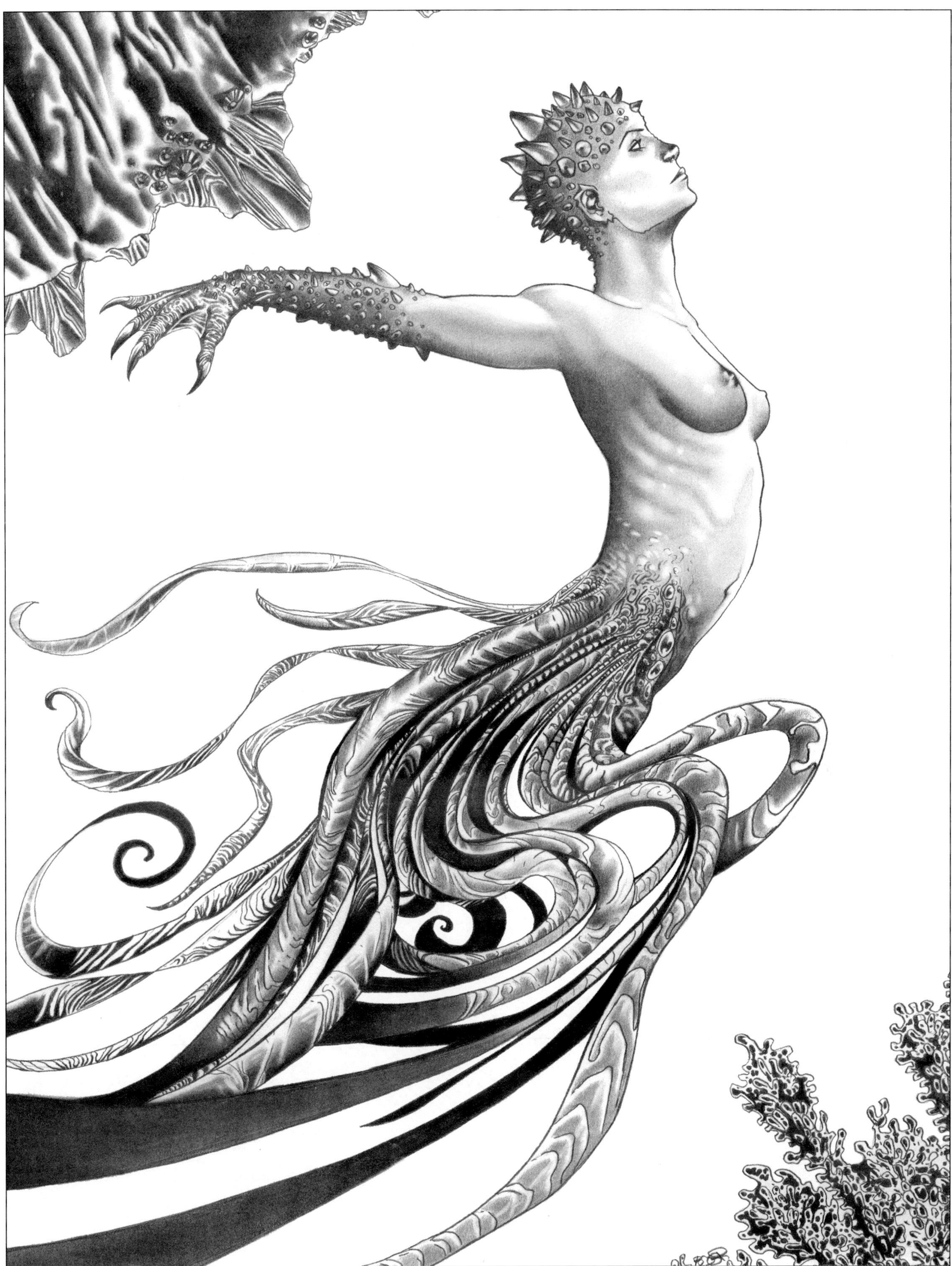

Luis Buci

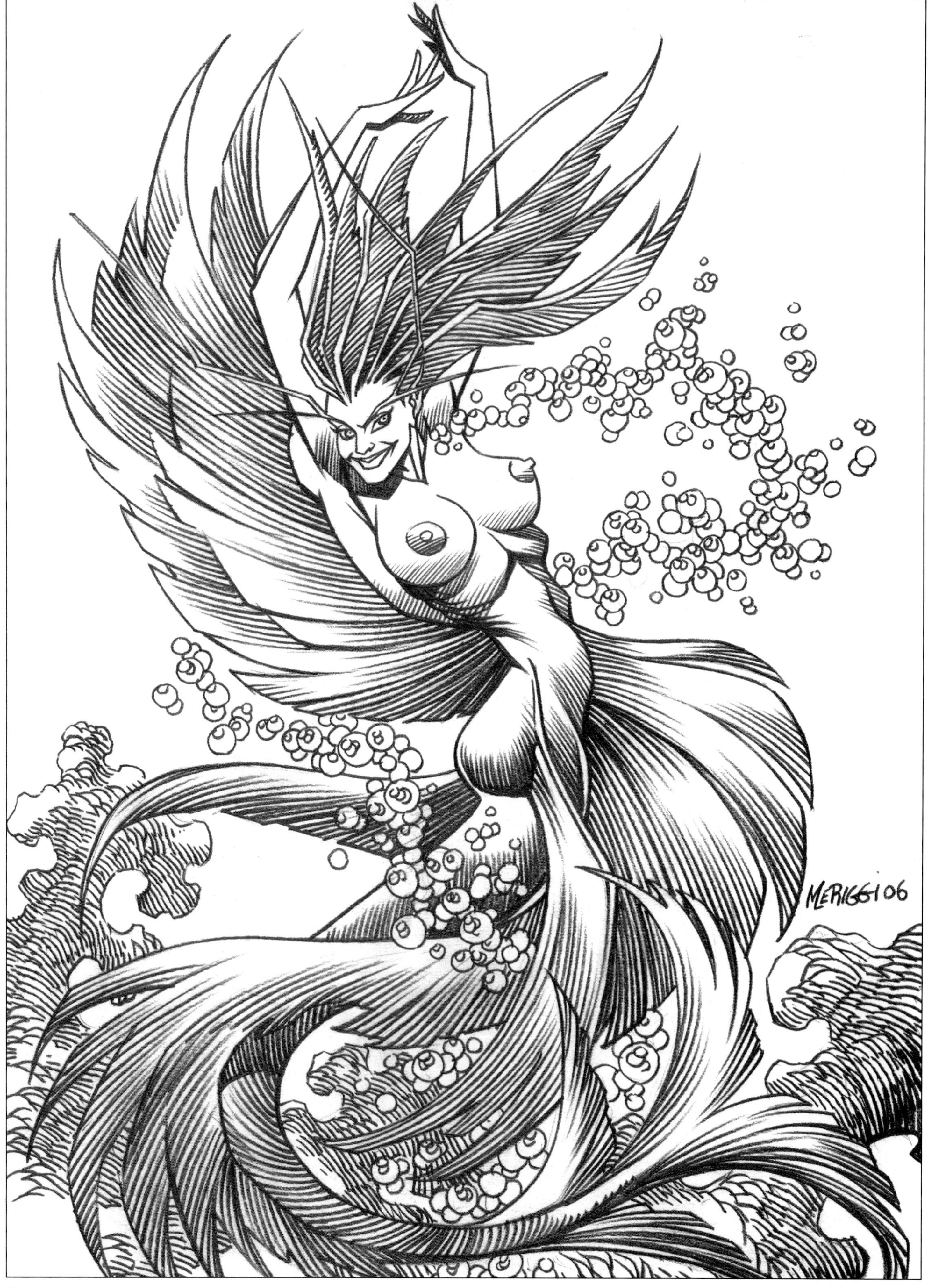
MERIGGI 06

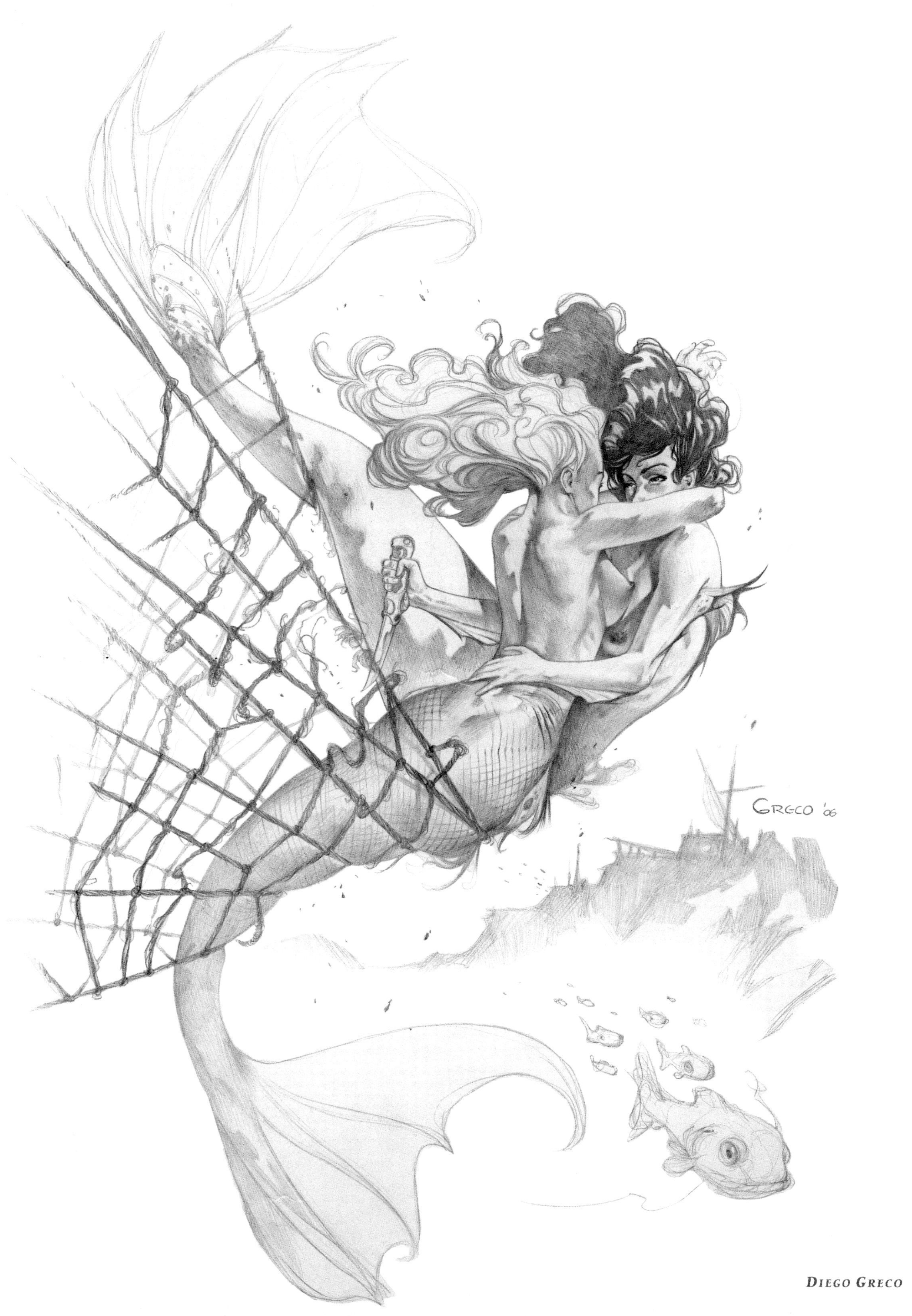

DIEGO GRECO

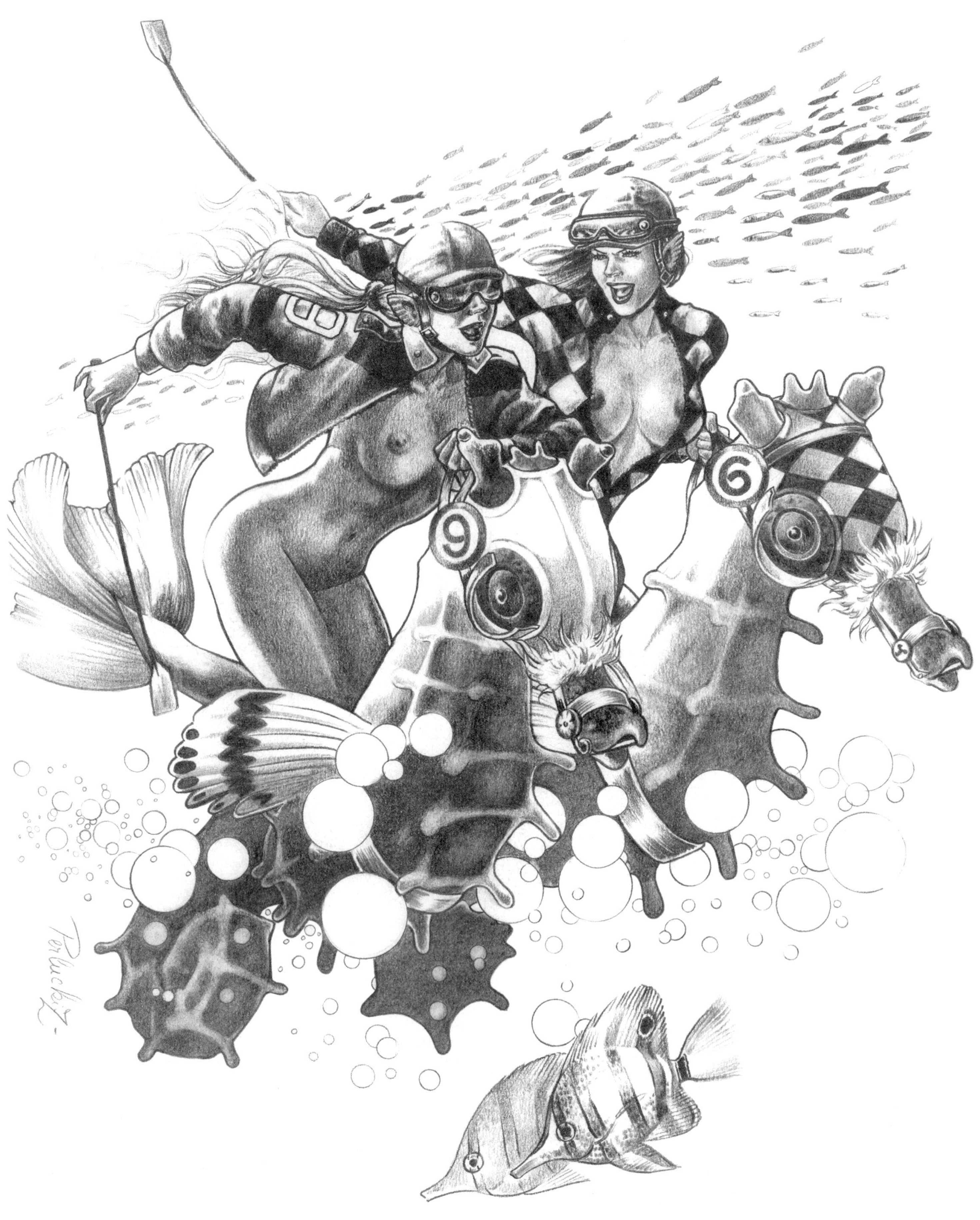

Perla Pilucki

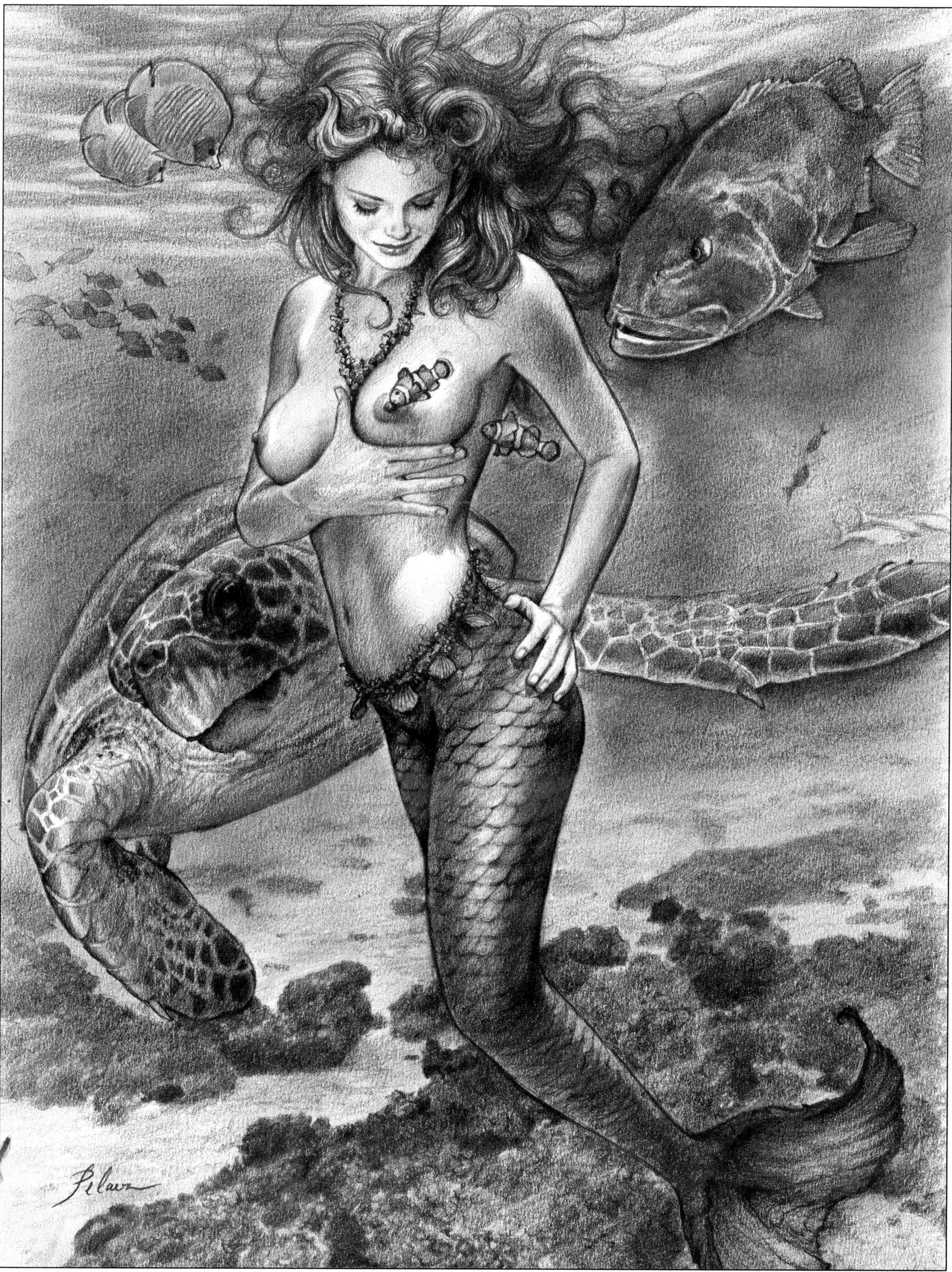

PELAEZ

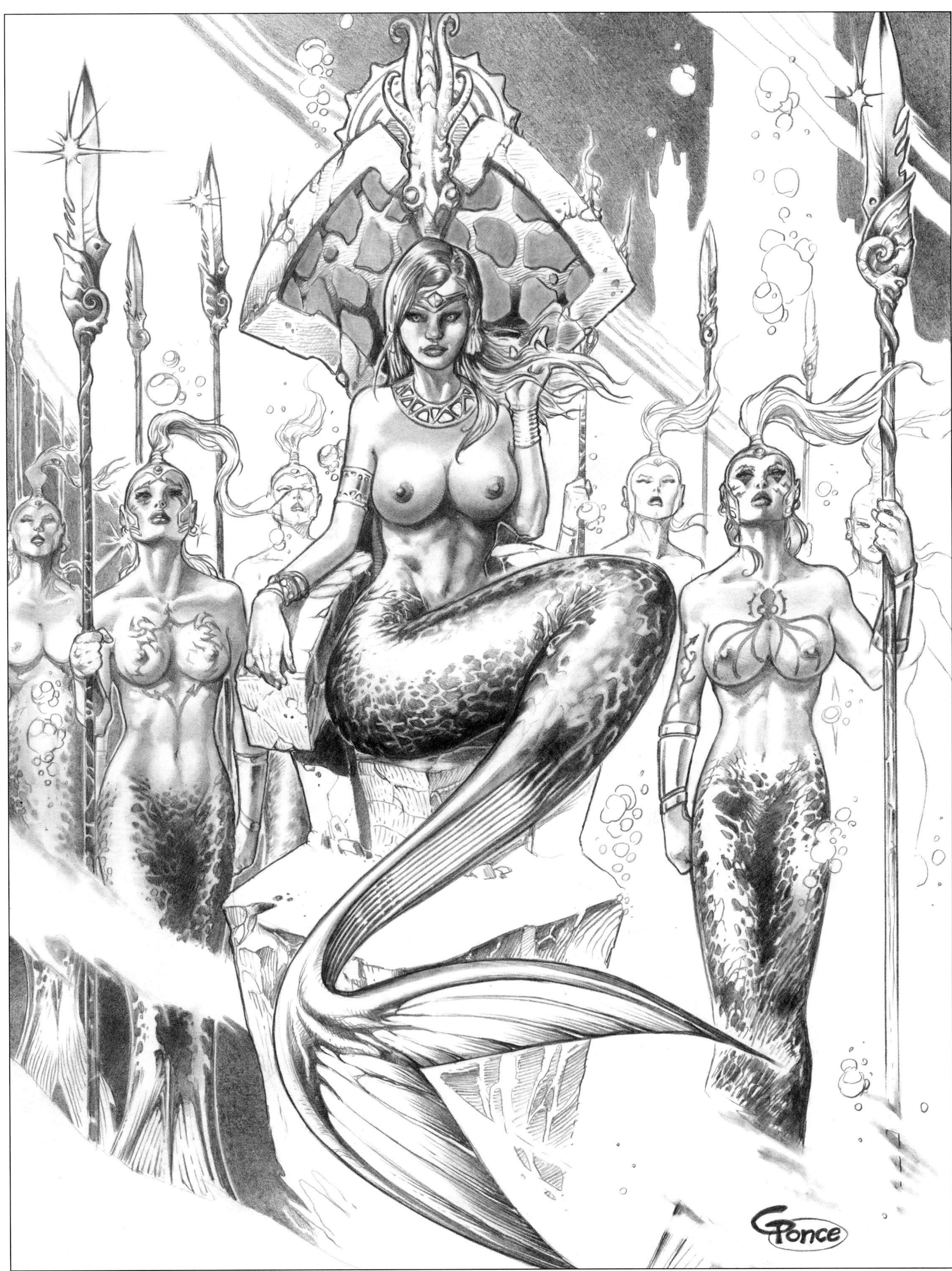
GPonce

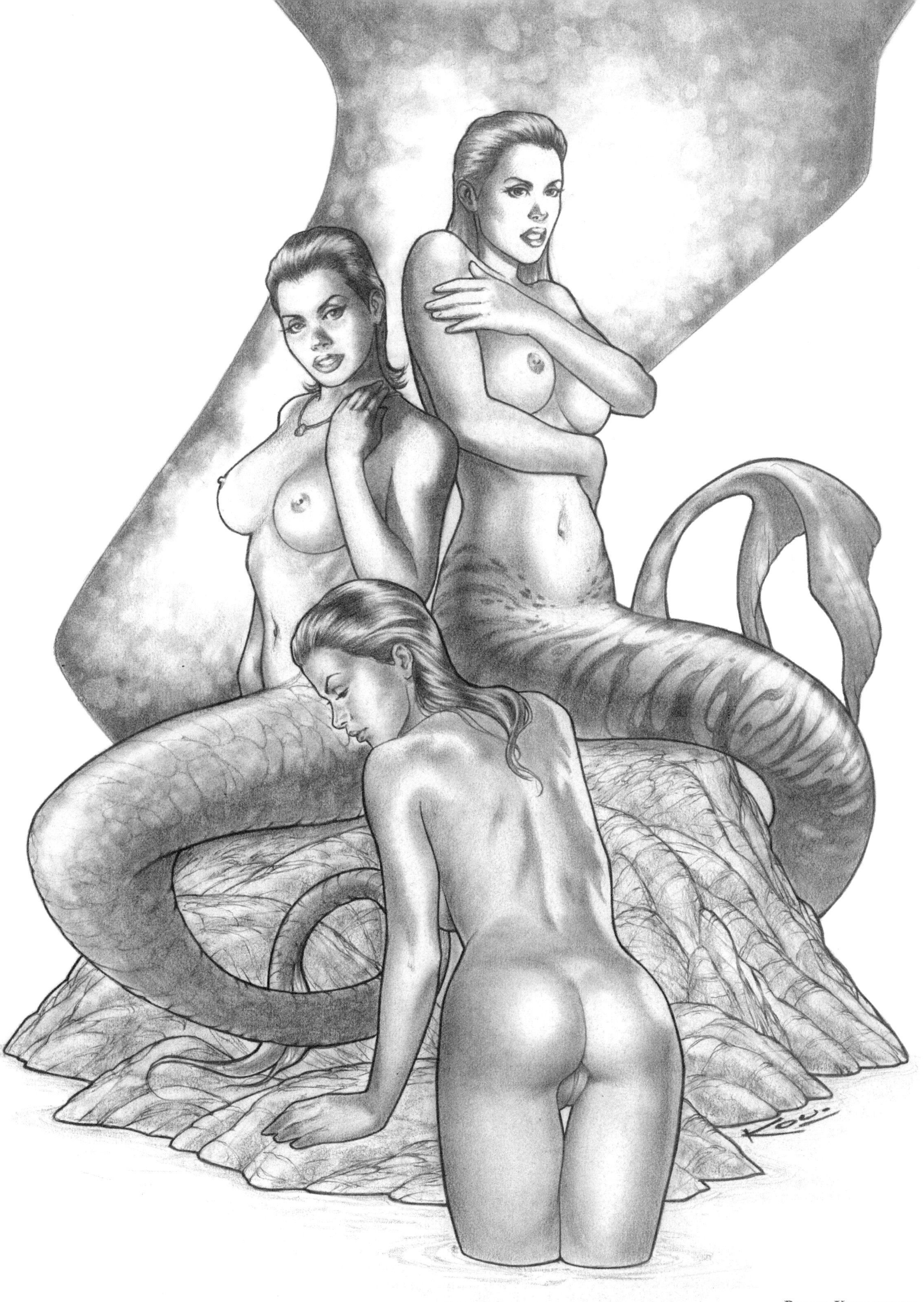

PABLO KOUSOVITIS

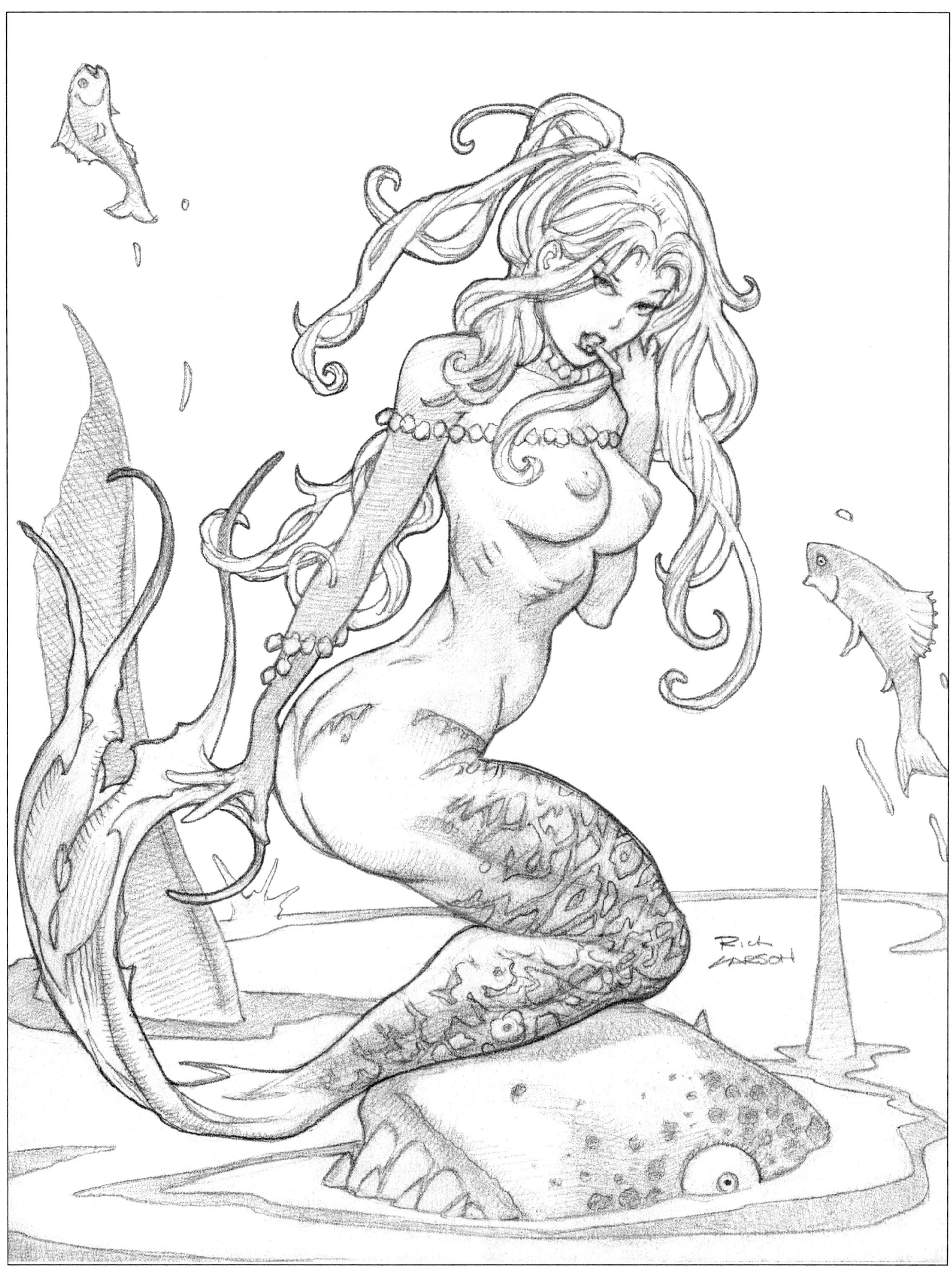

Rich Larson

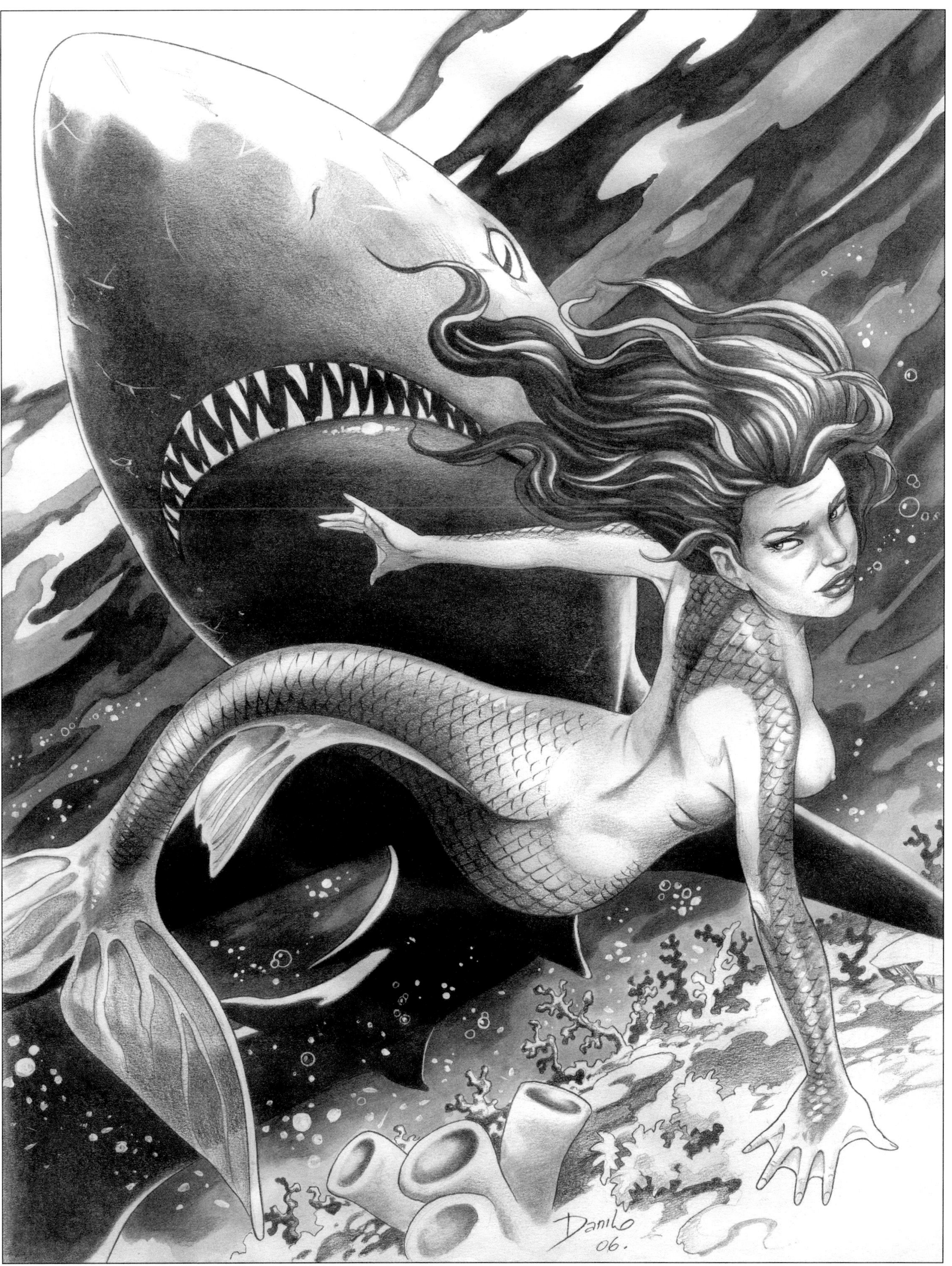

Danilo Guida

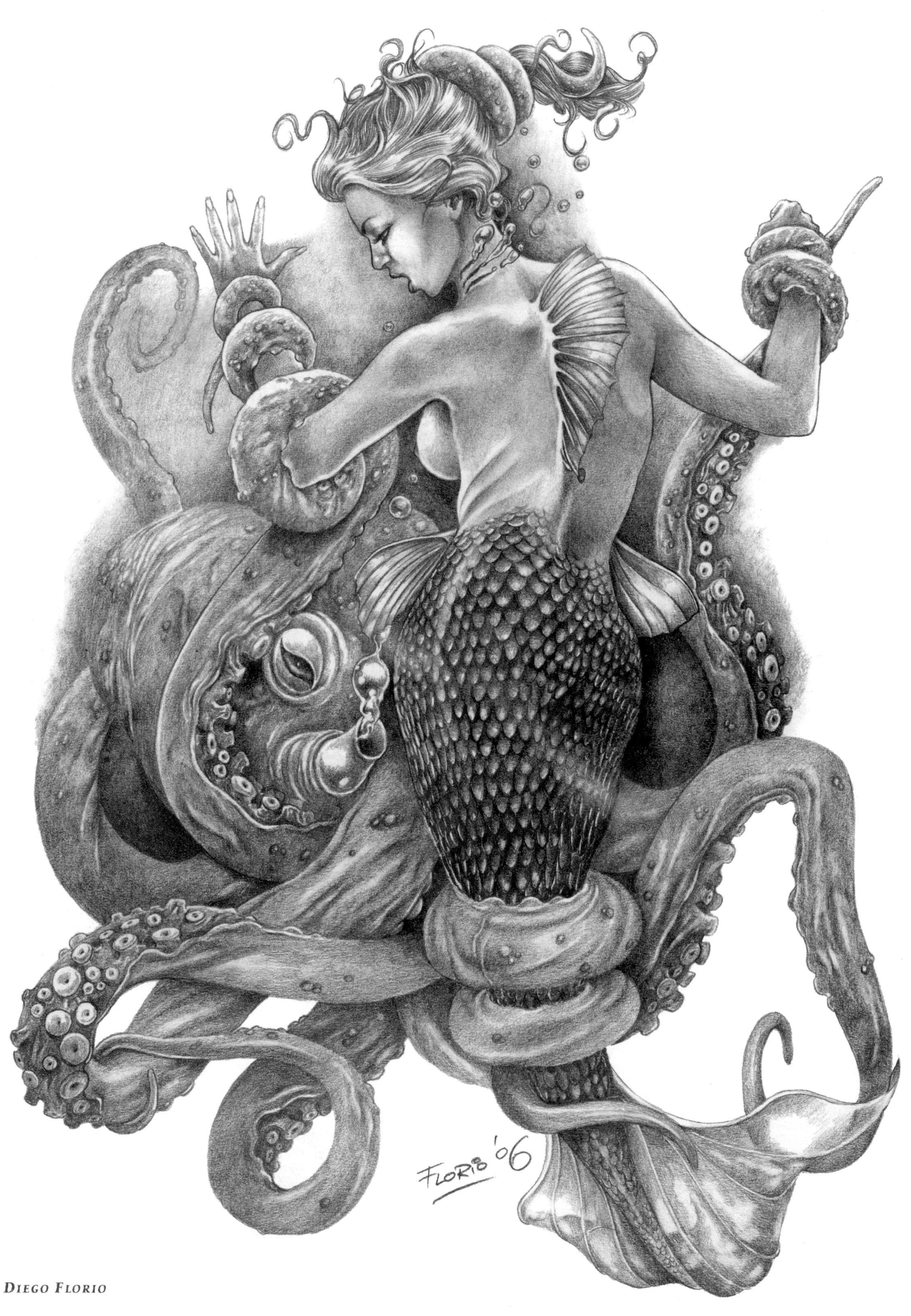

DIEGO FLORIO

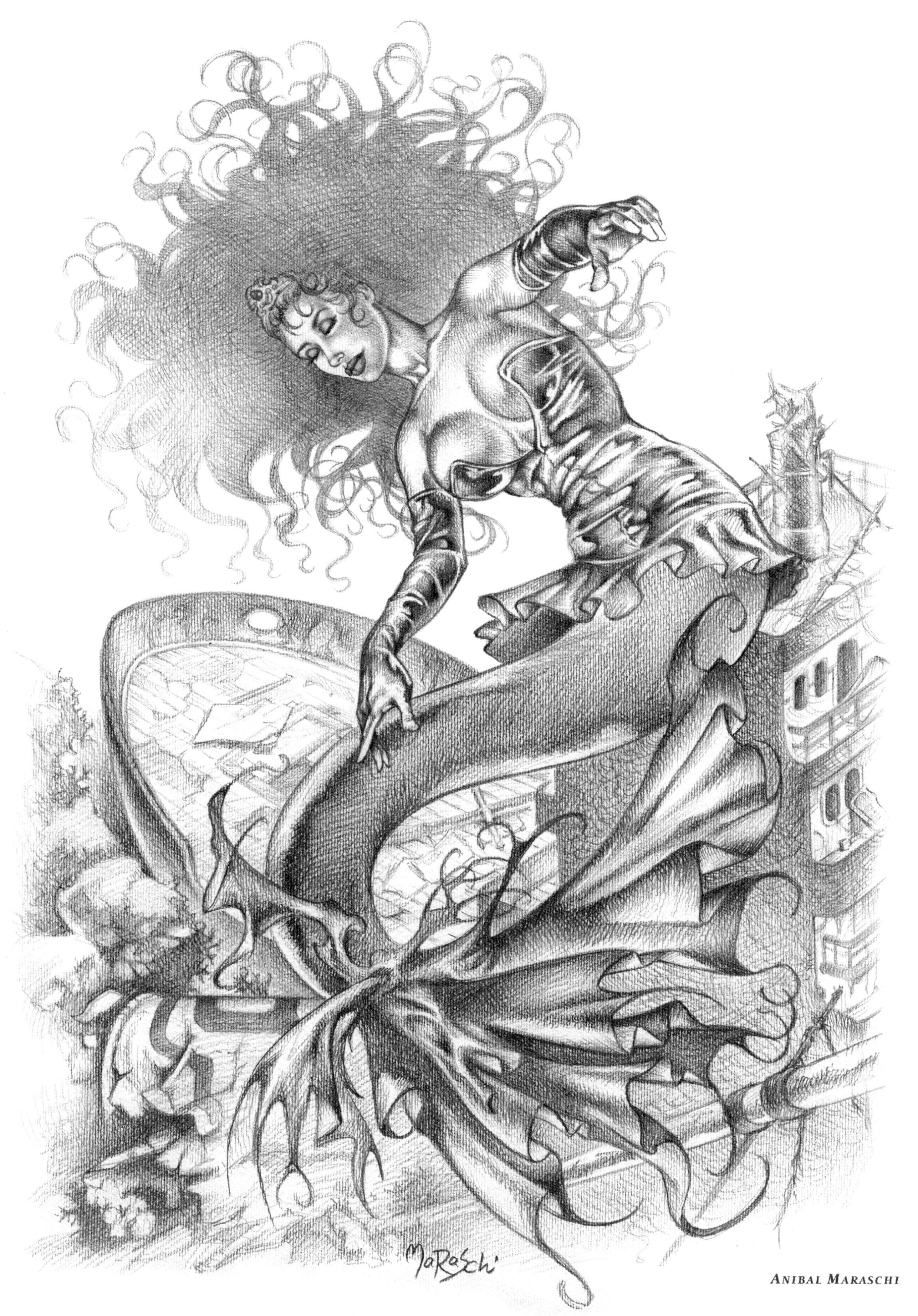

Anibal Maraschi

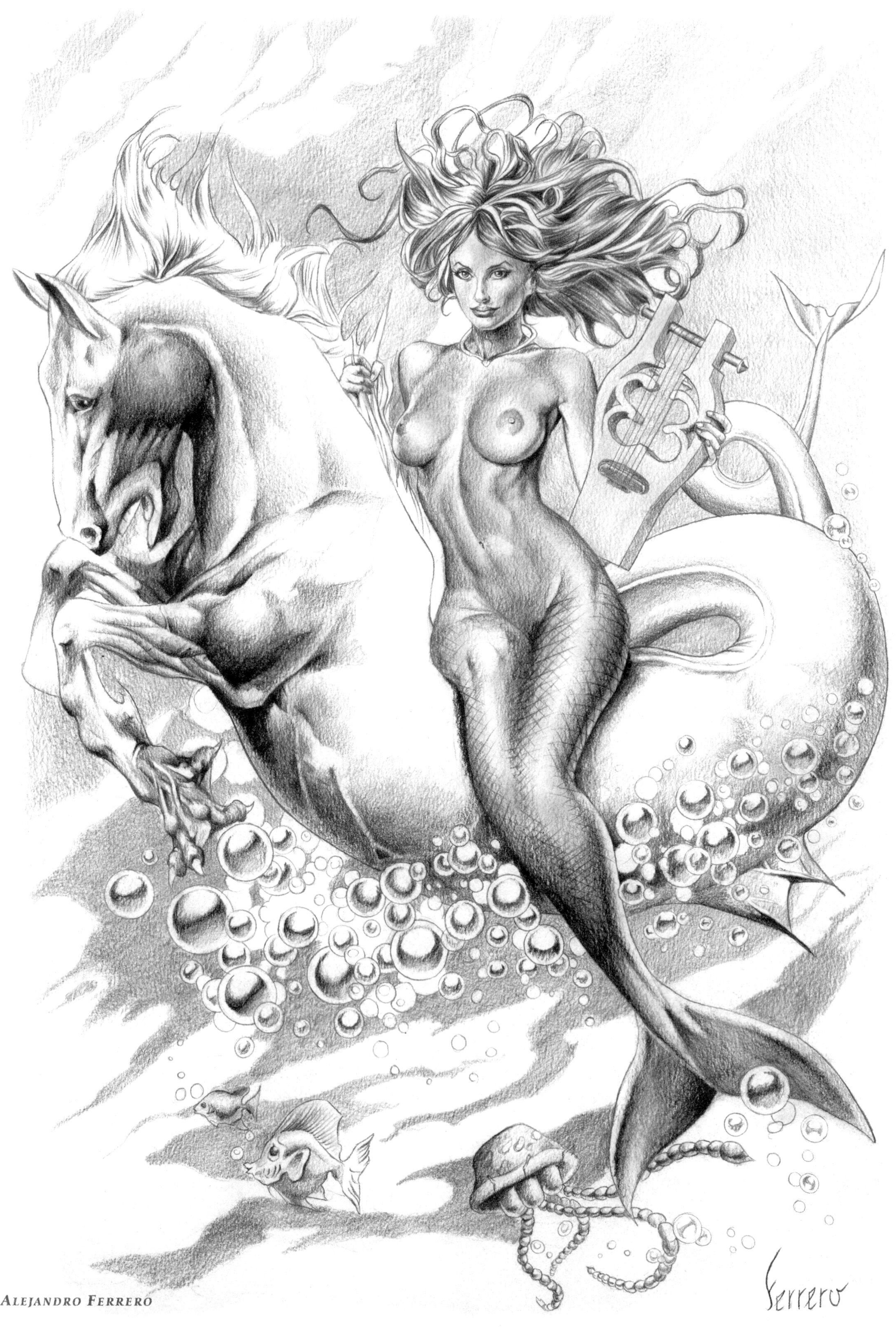

Alejandro Ferrero

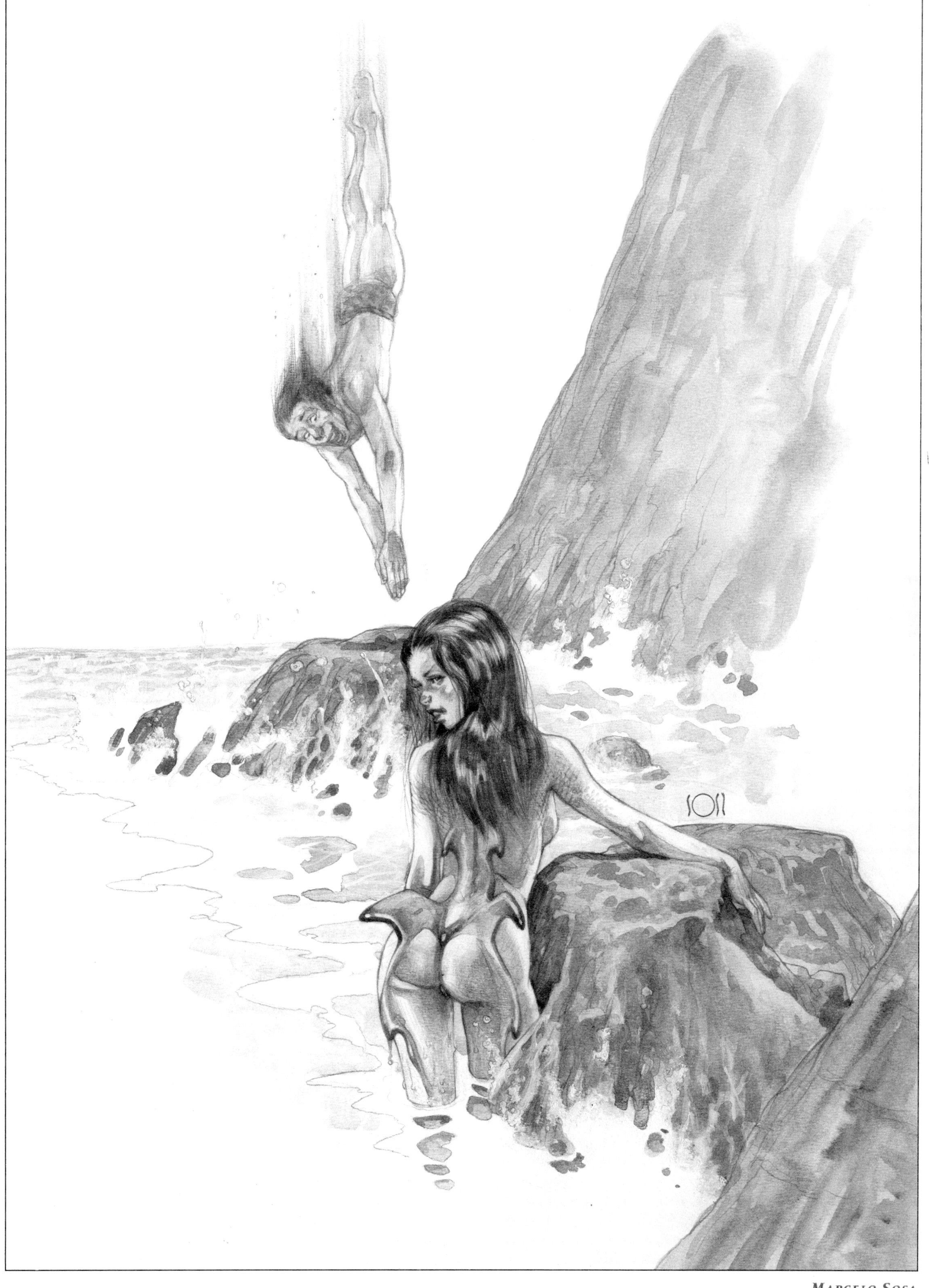

Marcelo Sosa

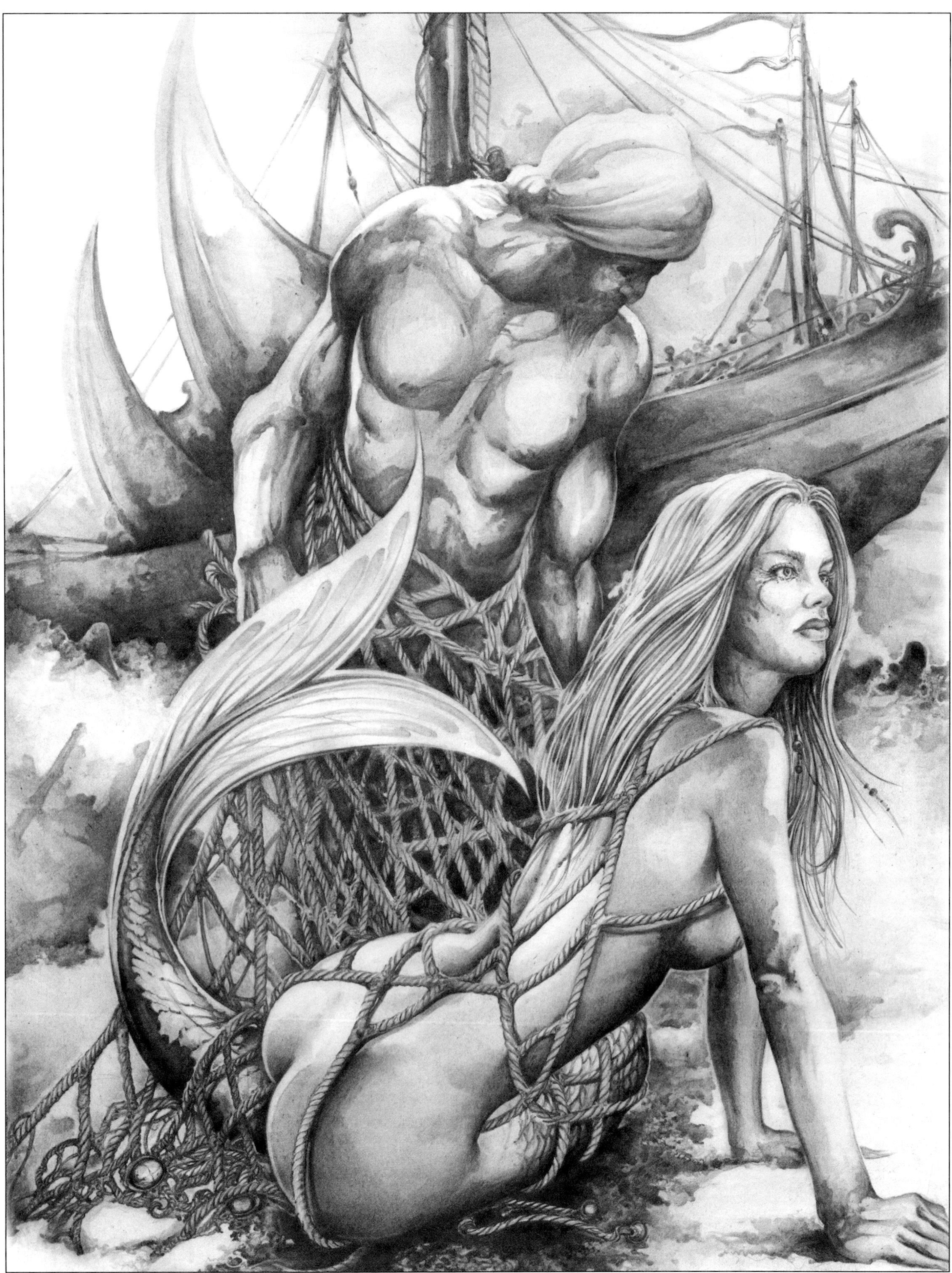

Aldo Perez

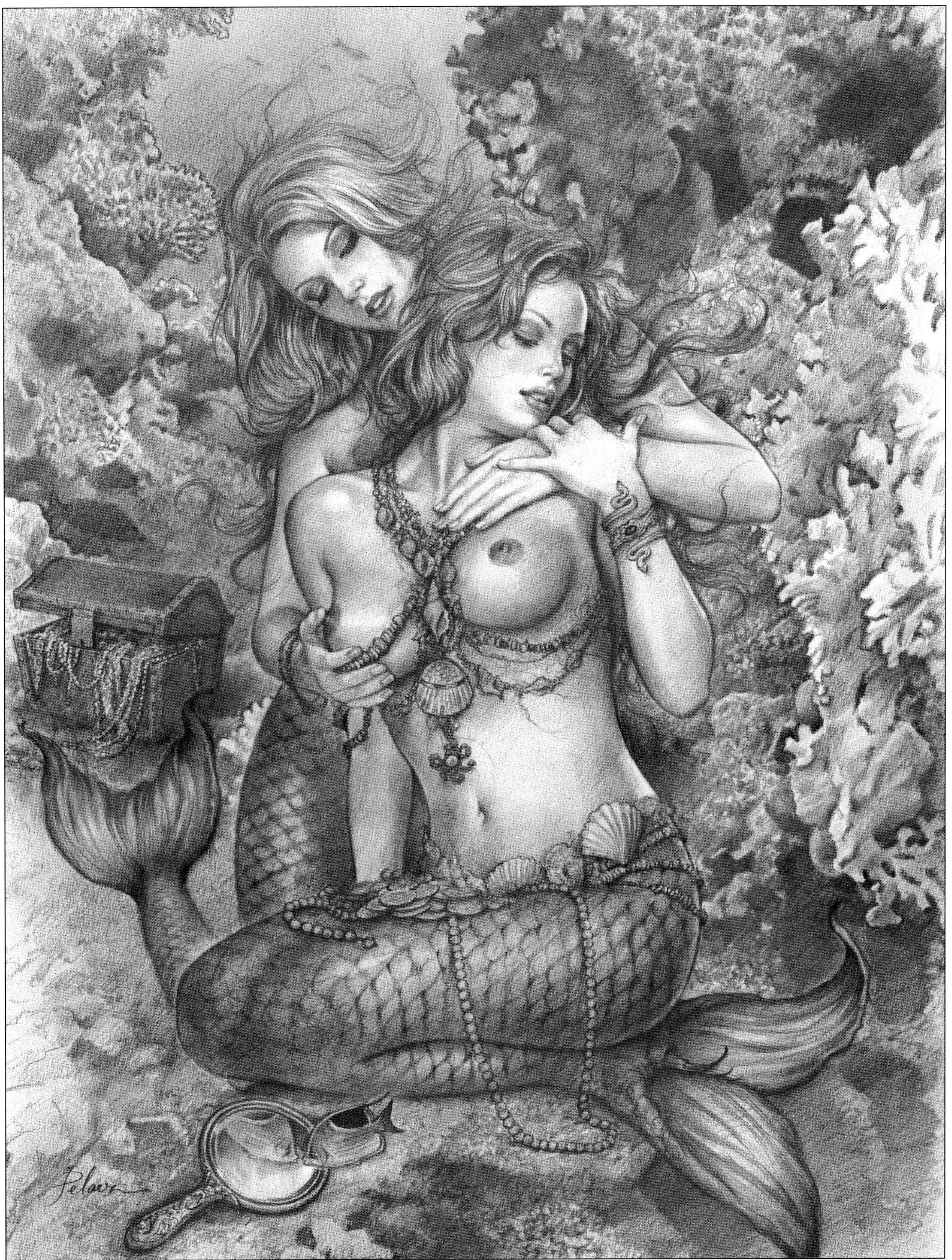

Pelaez

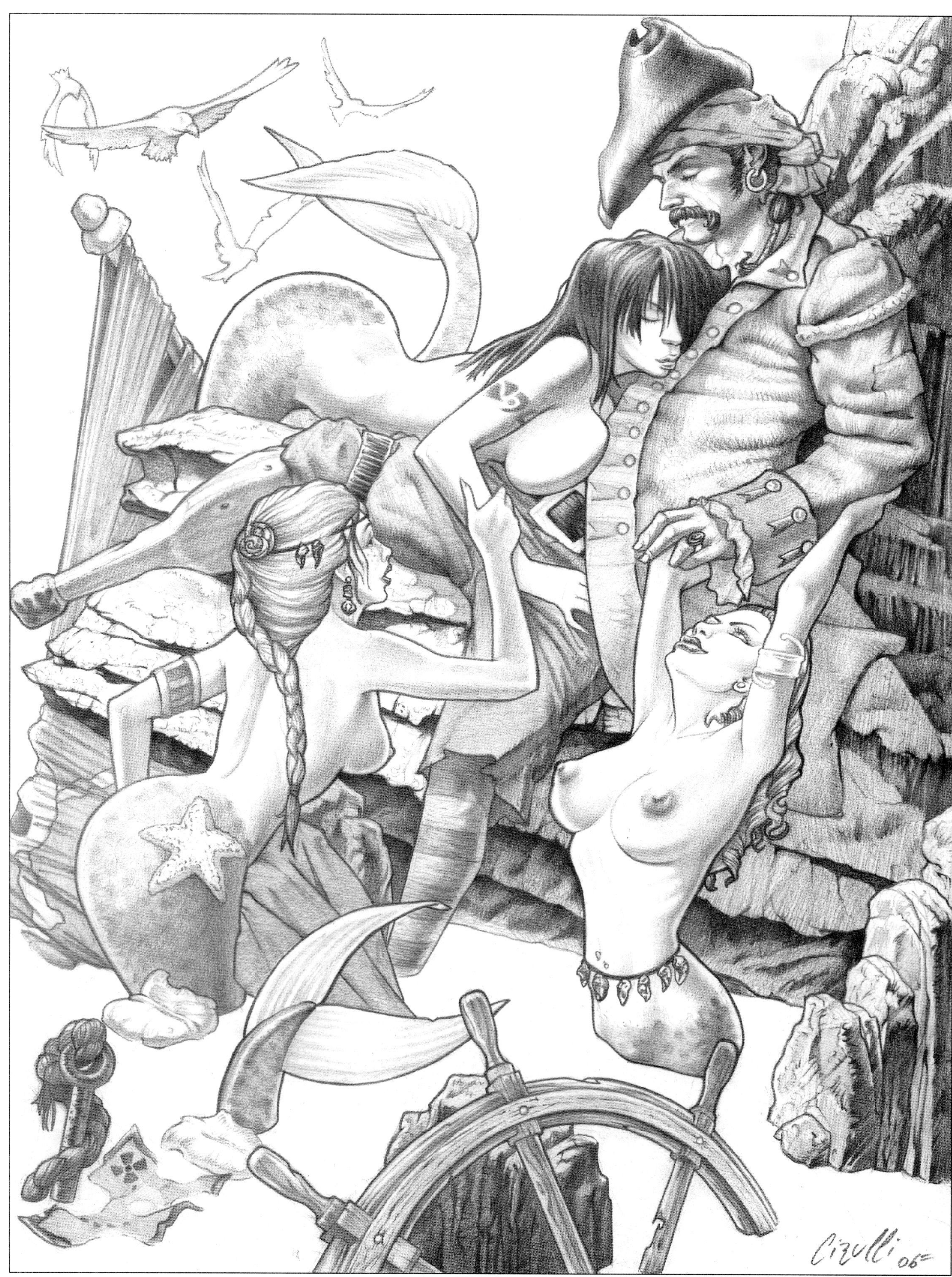

Diego Cirulli

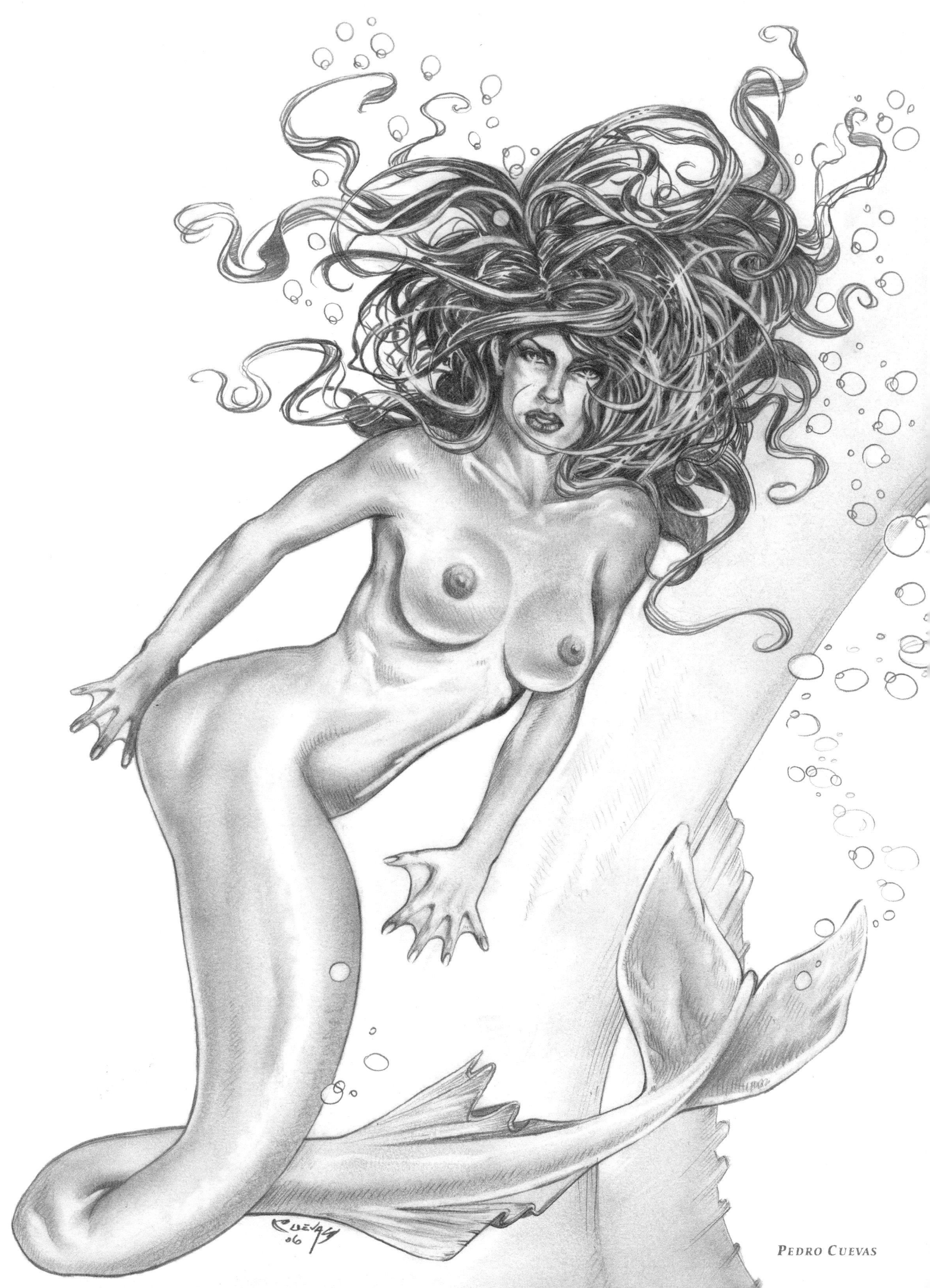

Pedro Cuevas

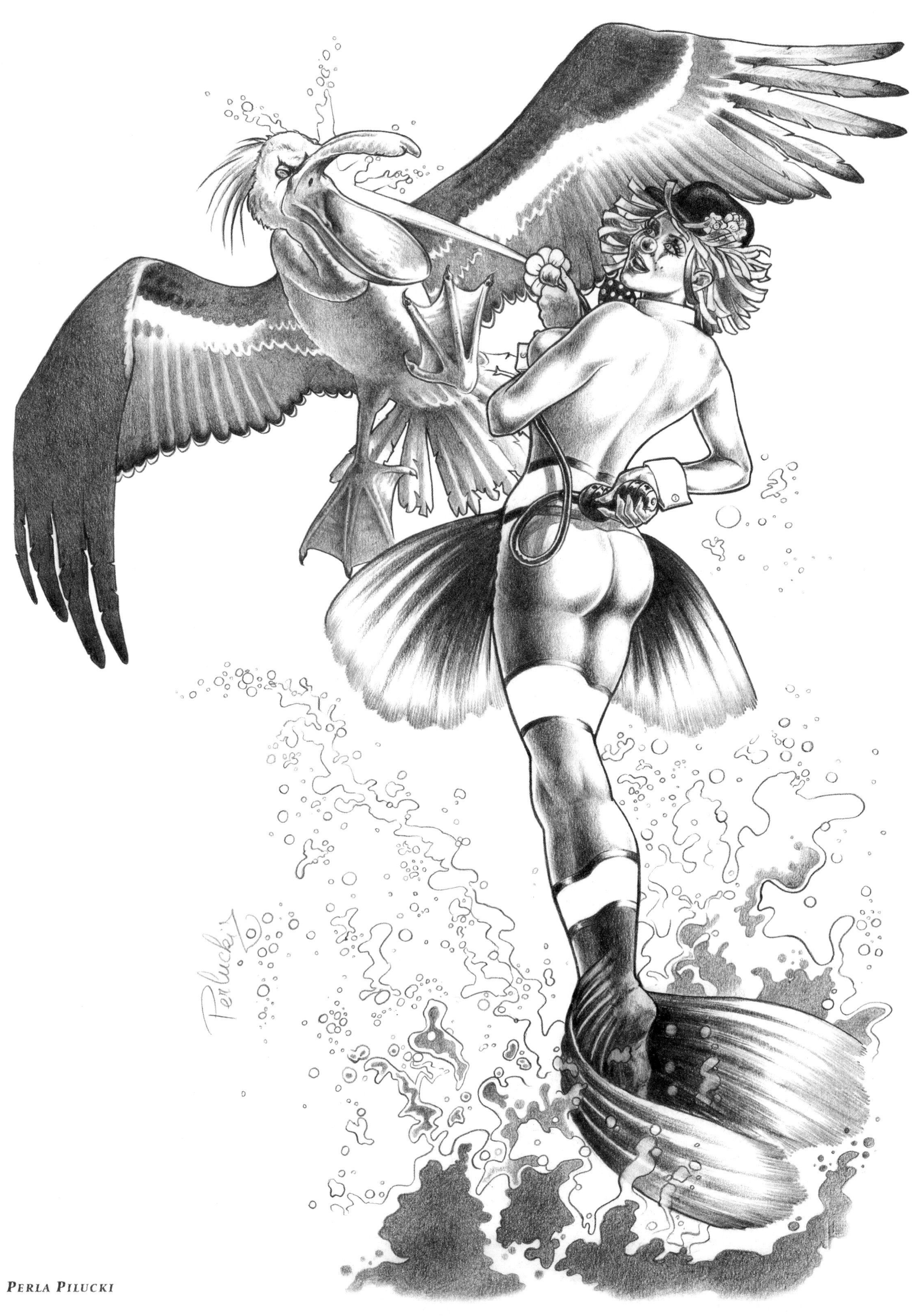

Perla Pilucki

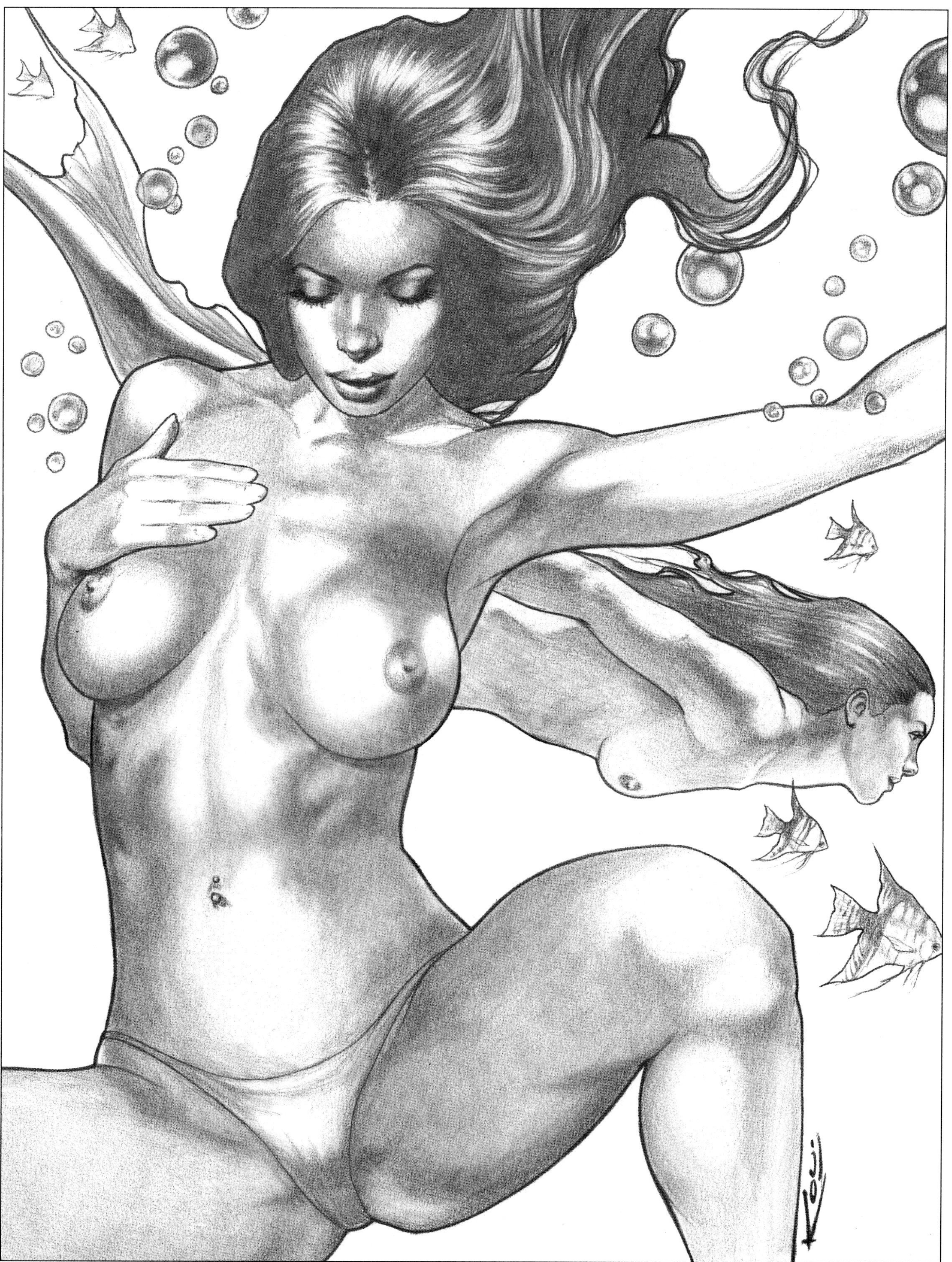

Pablo Kousovitis

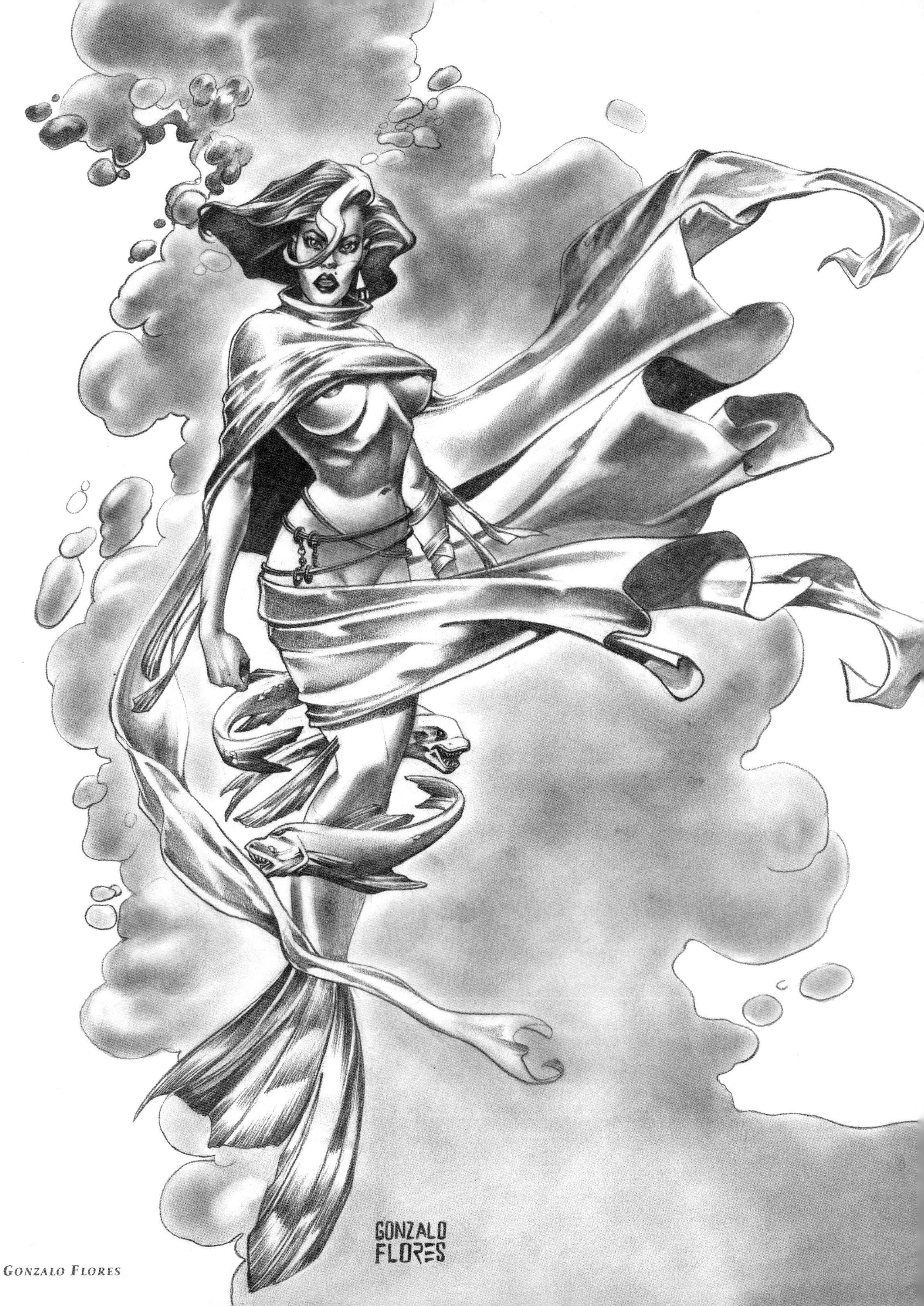

Gonzalo Flores

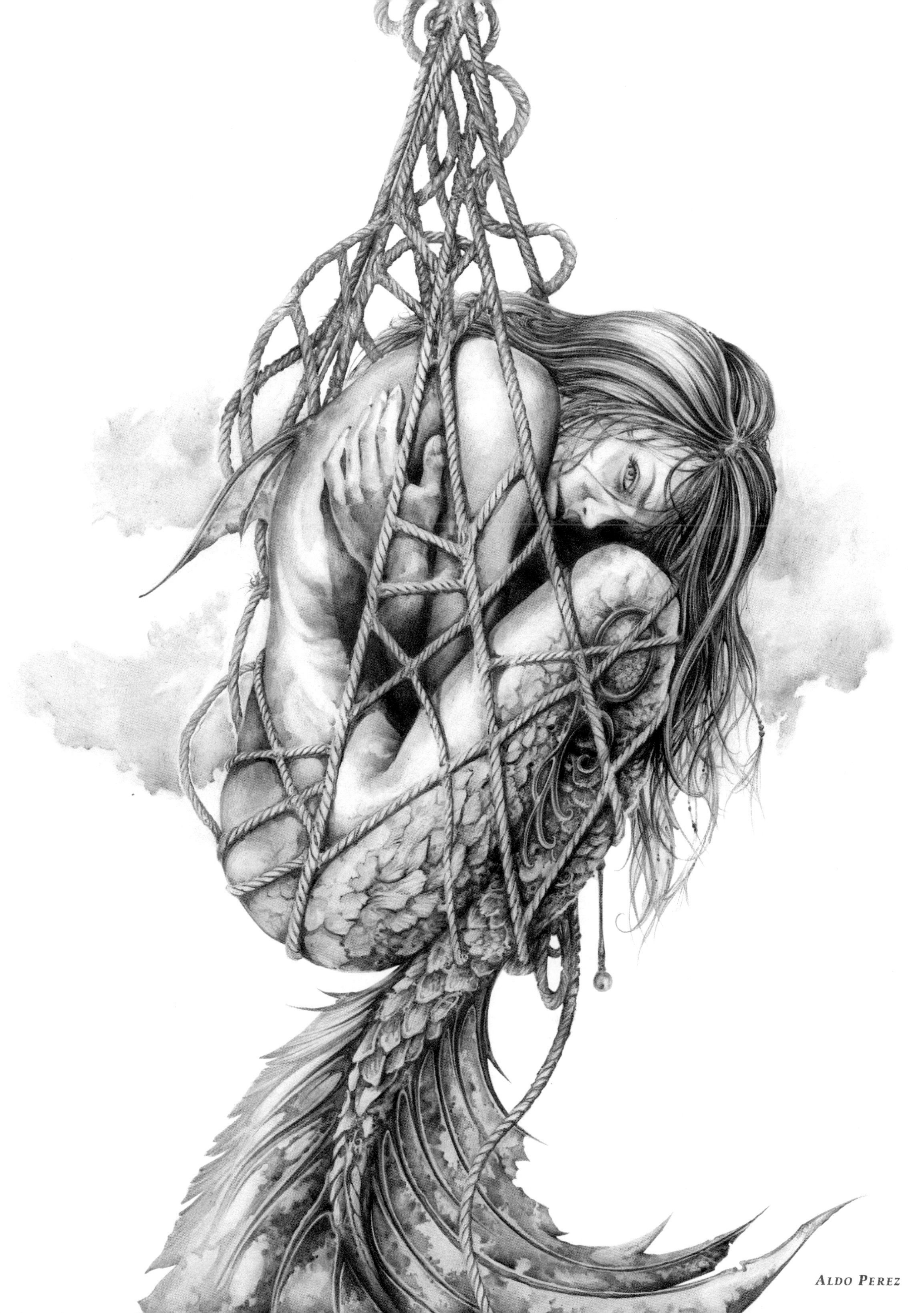

Aldo Perez

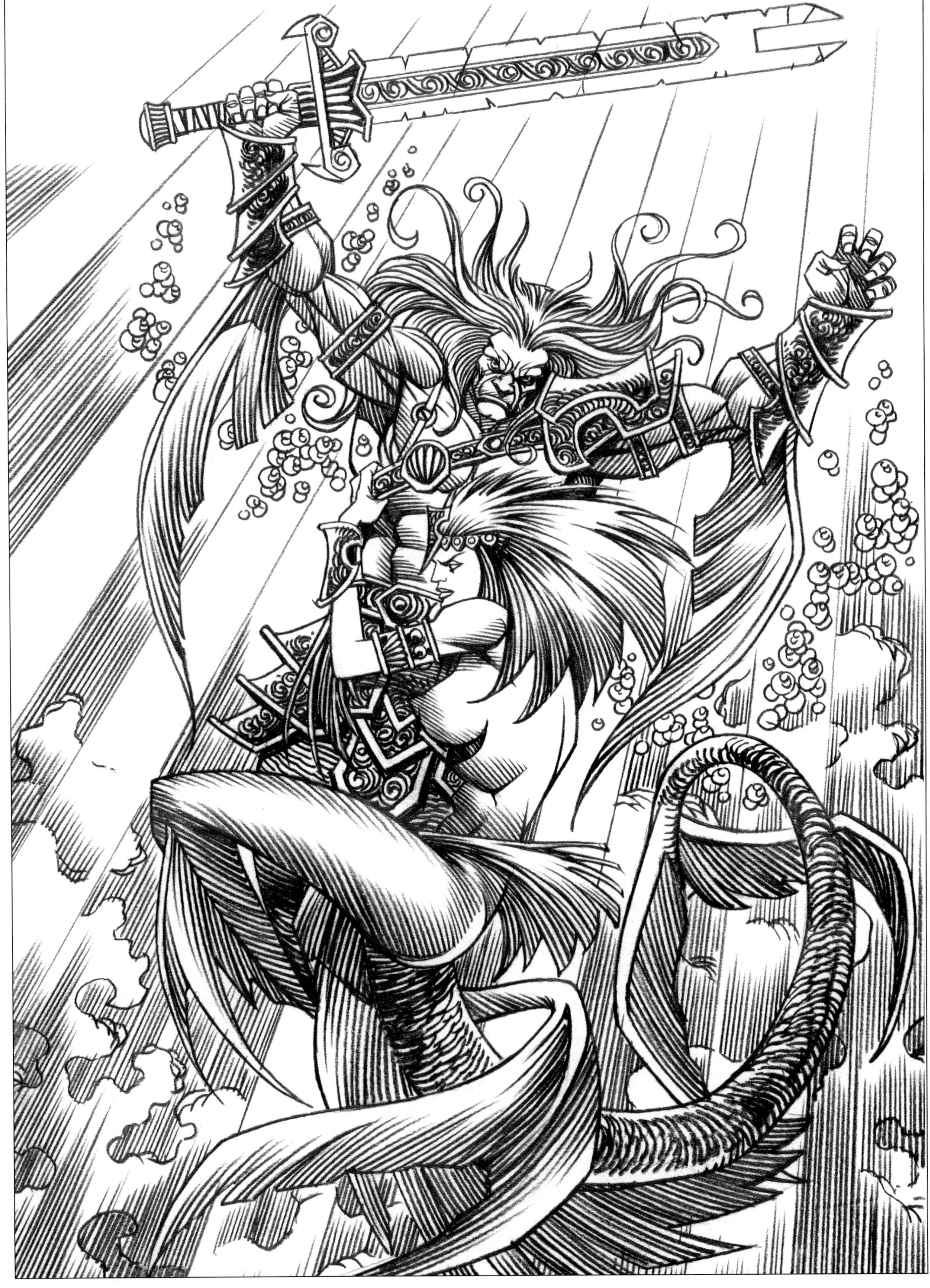

Ruben Meriggi

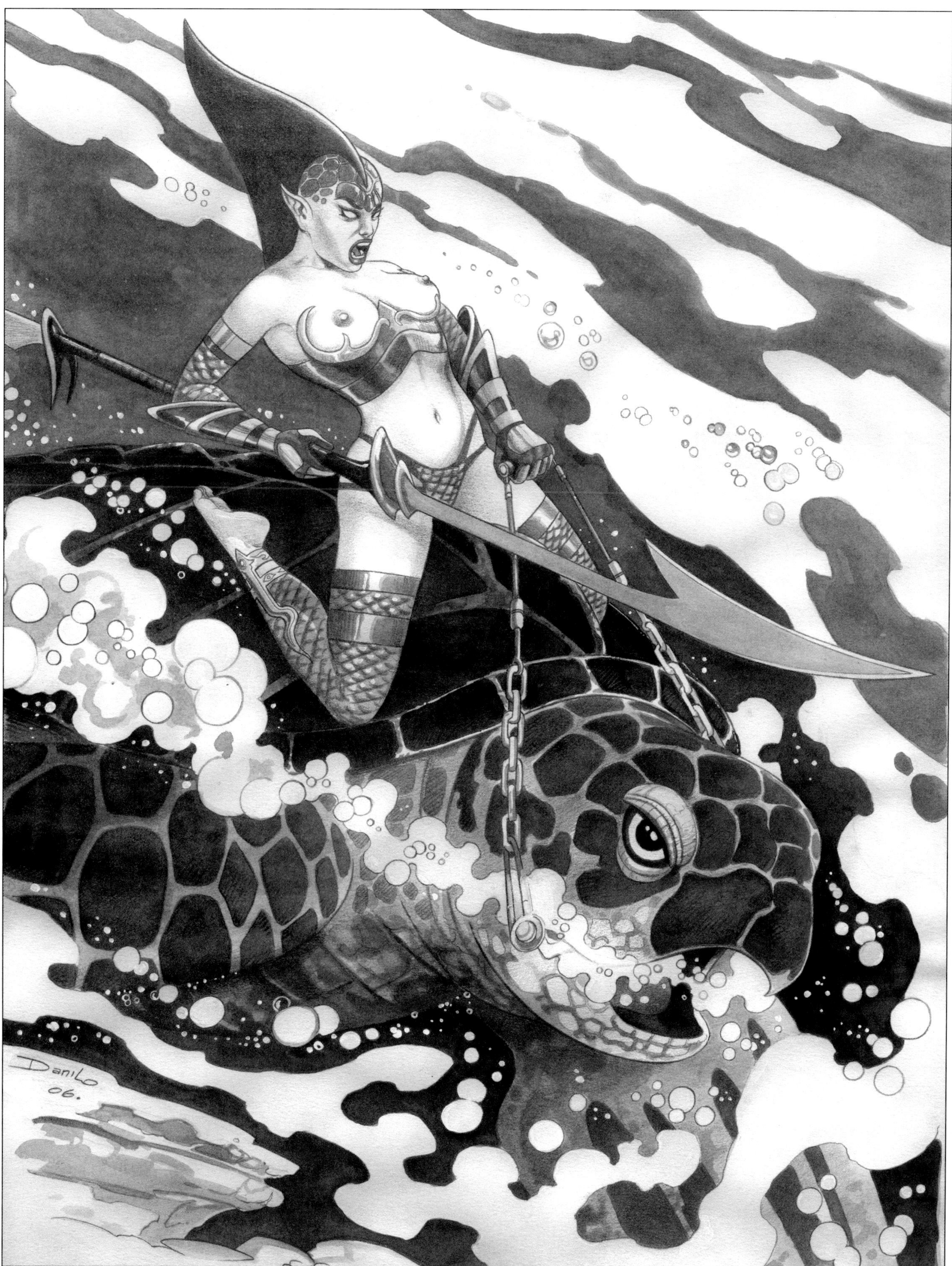

Danilo Guida

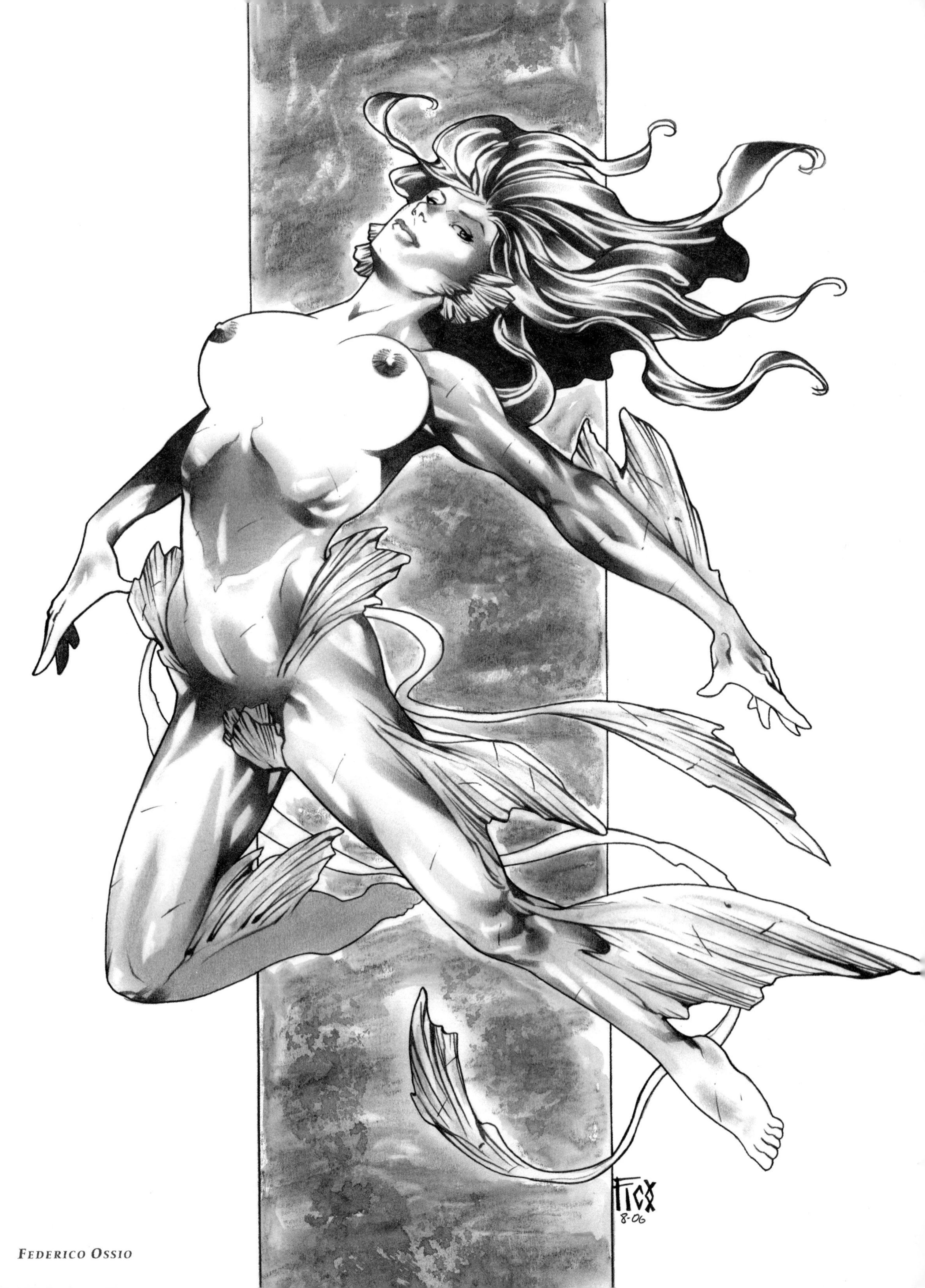

Federico Ossio

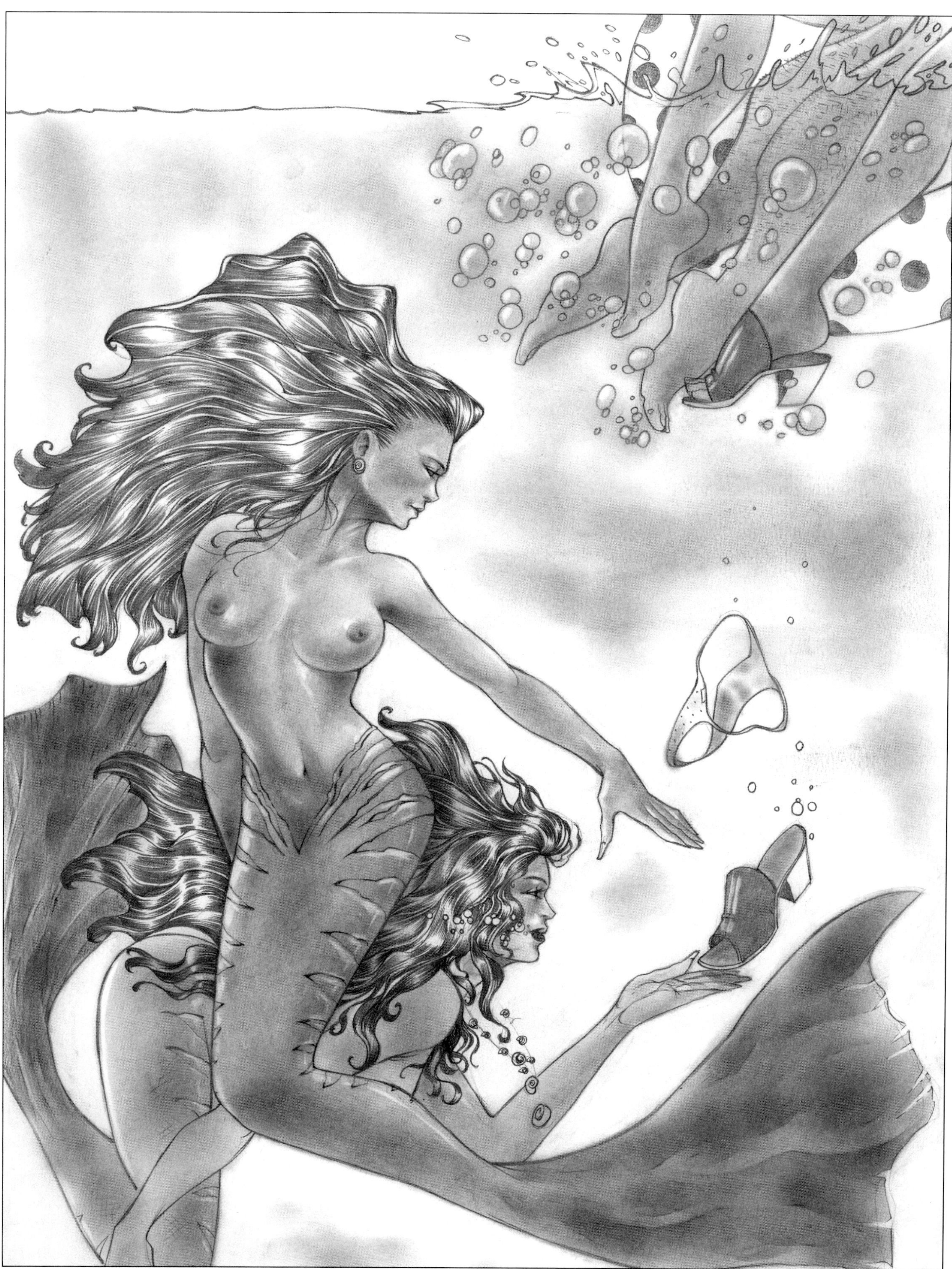

J.L. Czerniawski

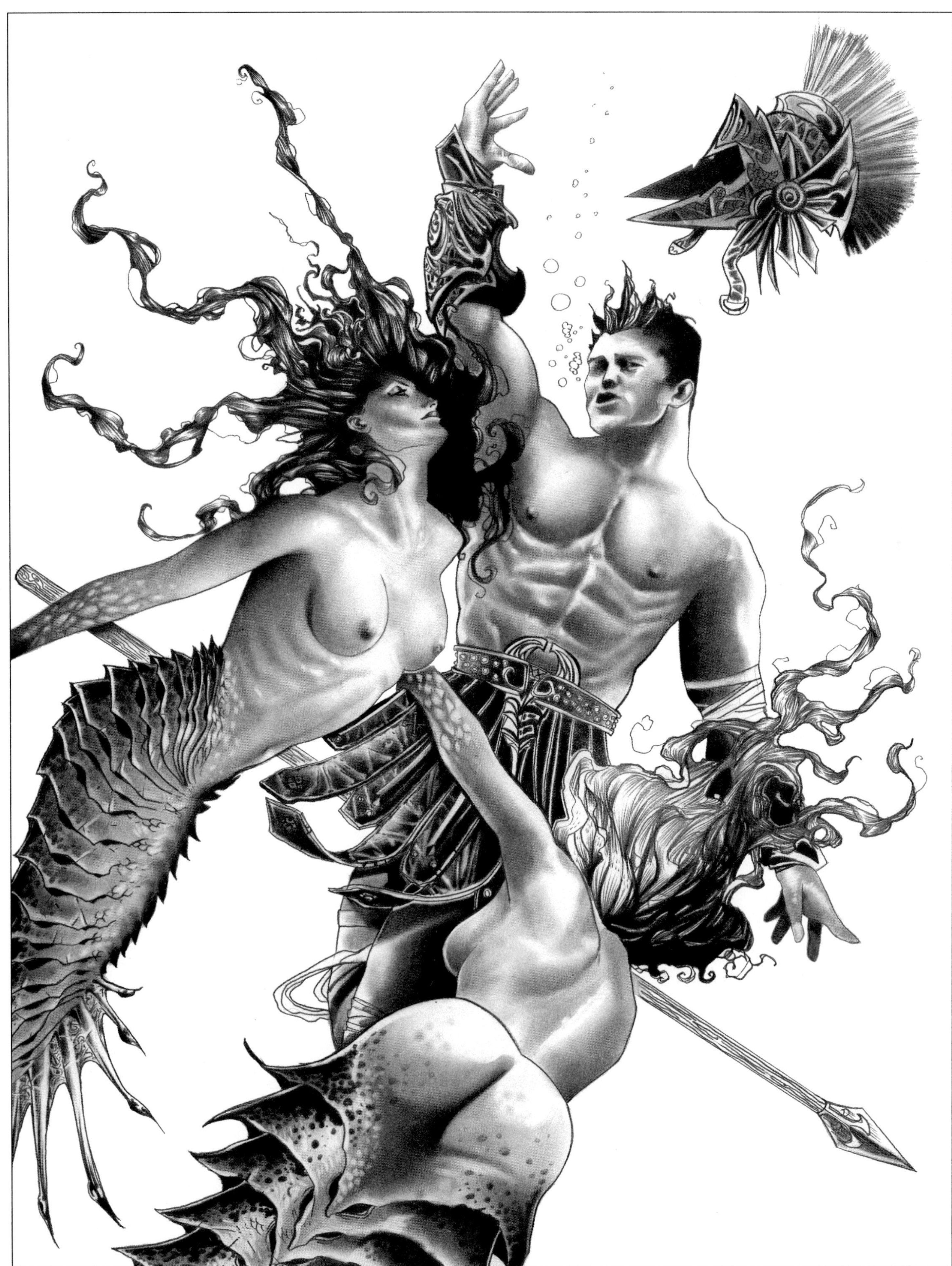

Luis Buci

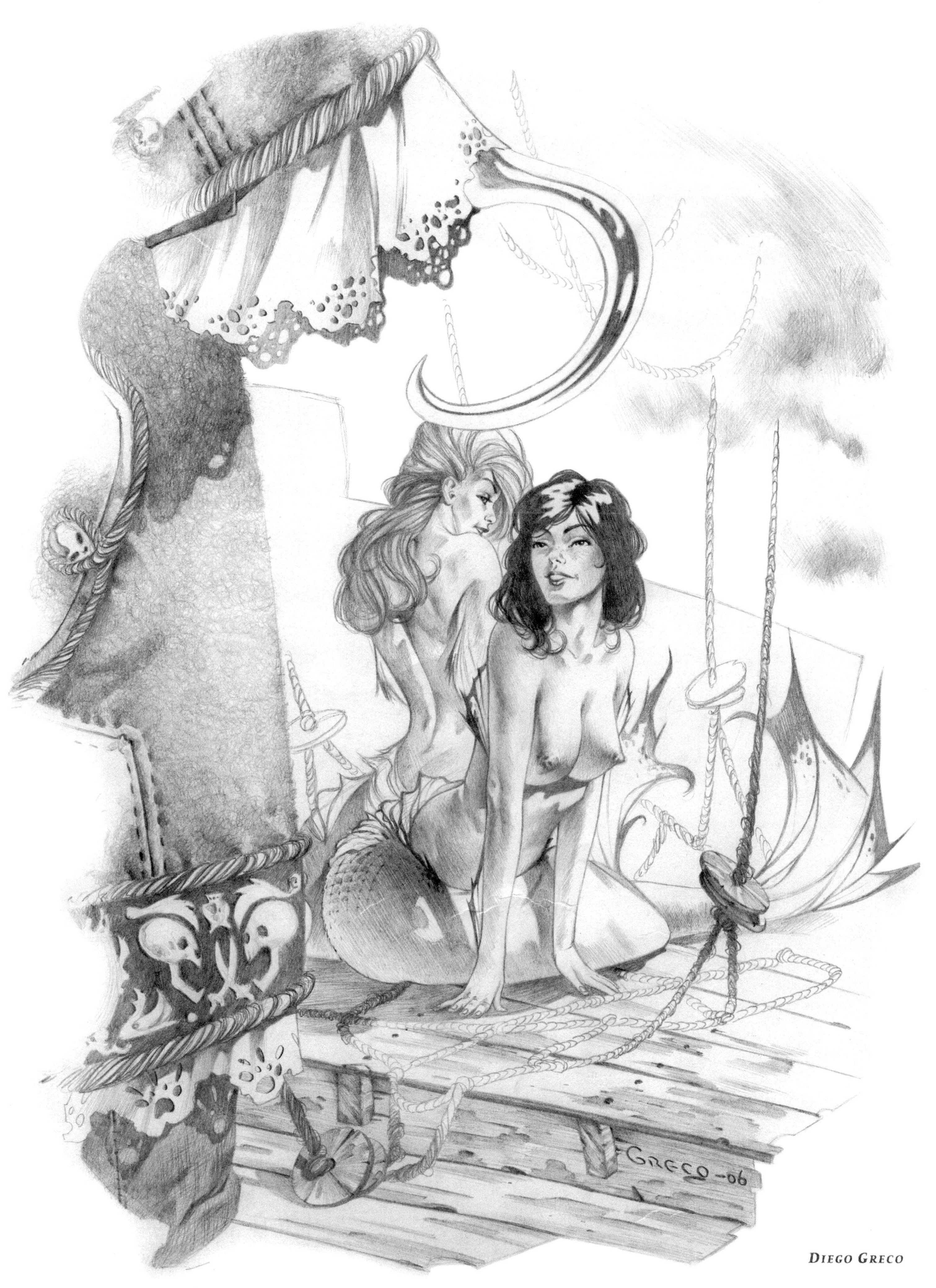

Diego Greco

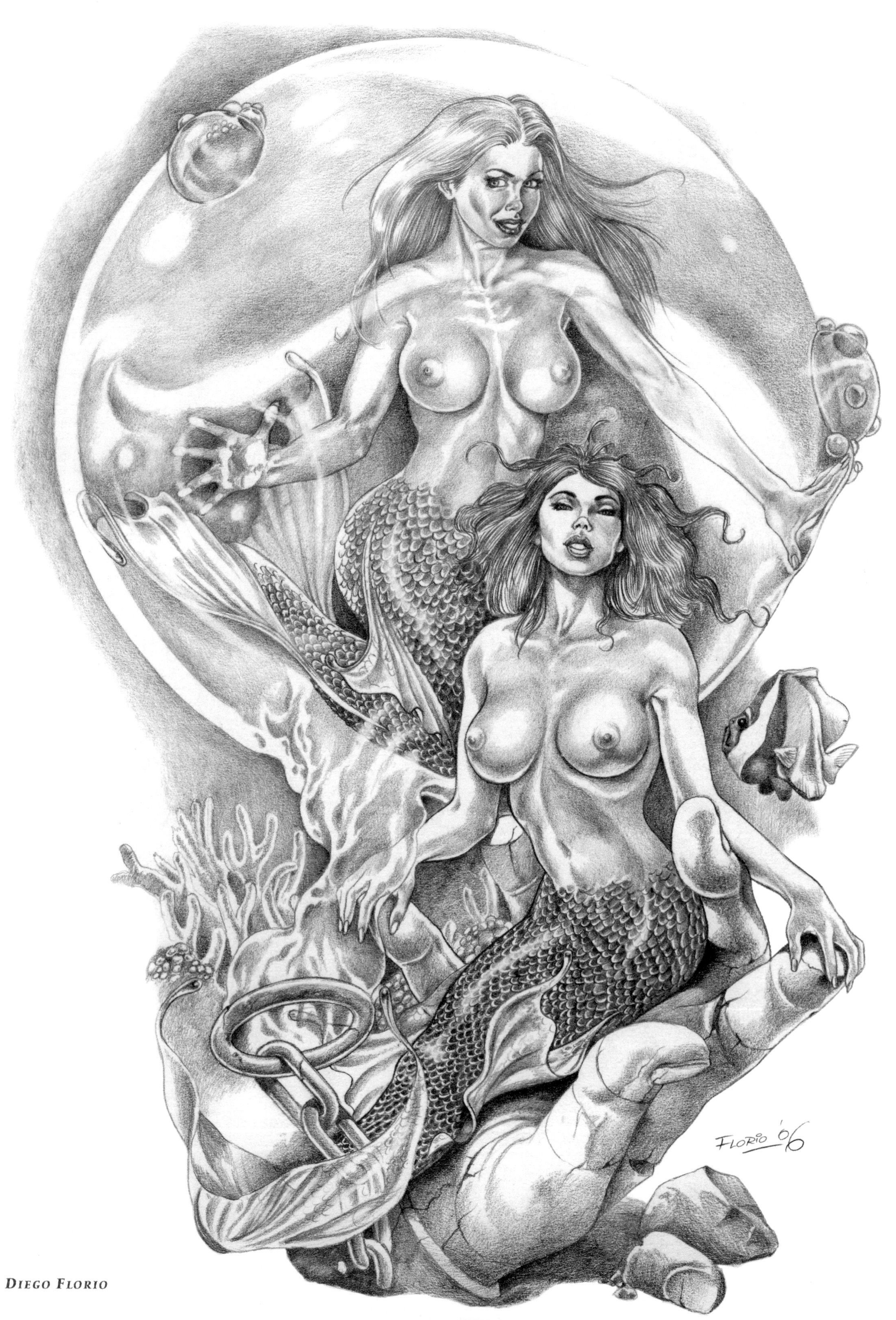

DIEGO FLORIO

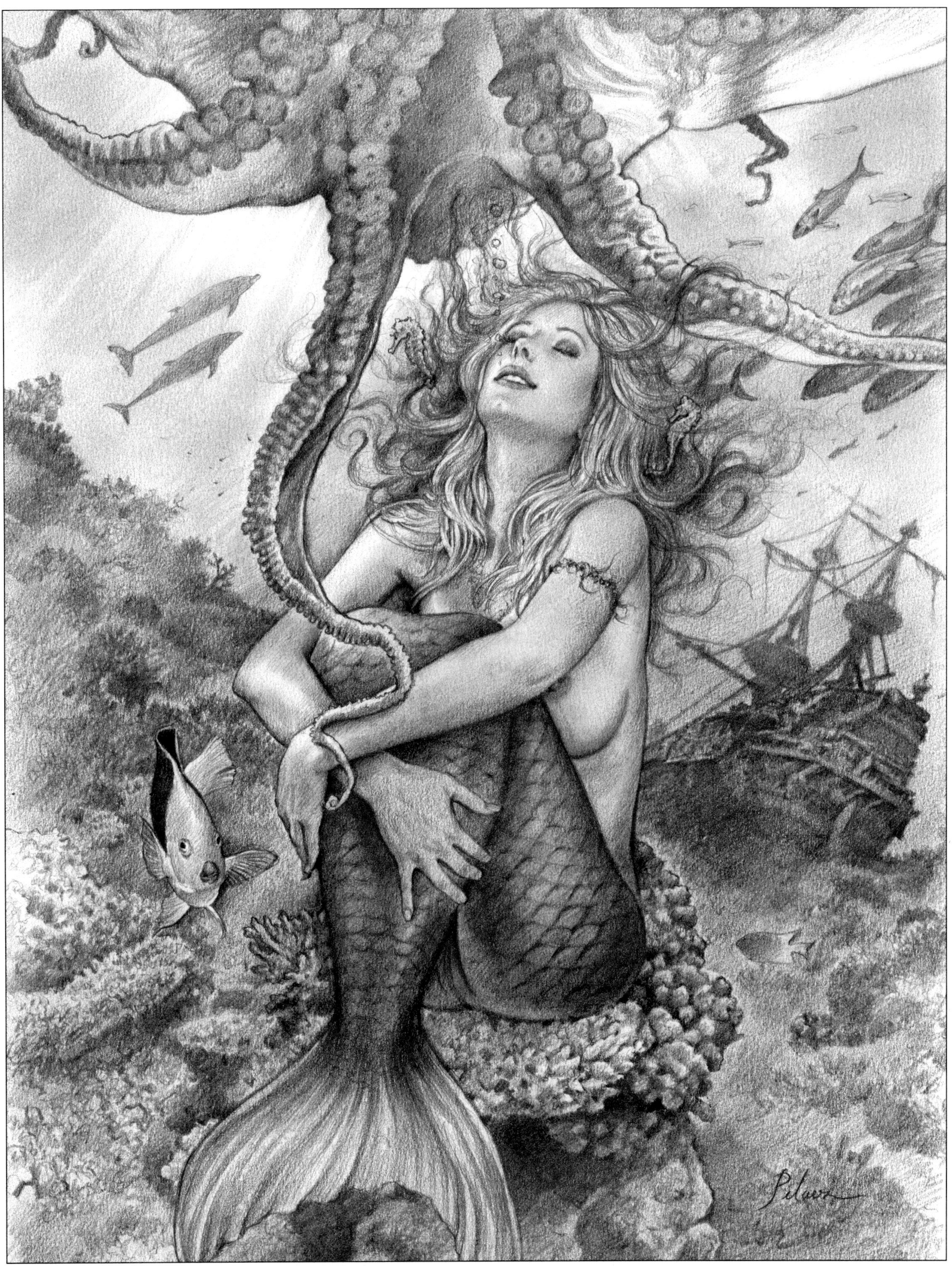
Pelaez

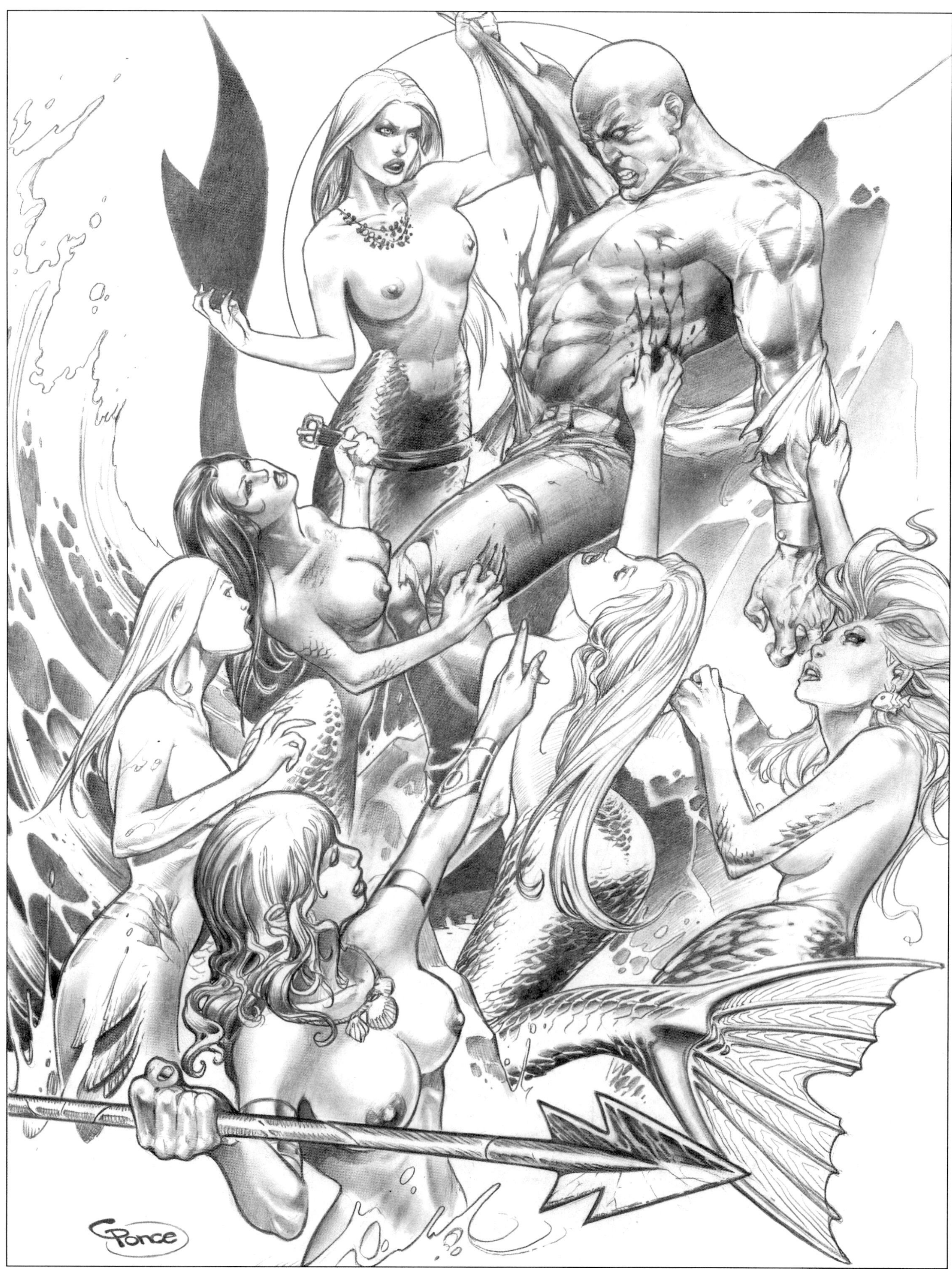

German Ponce

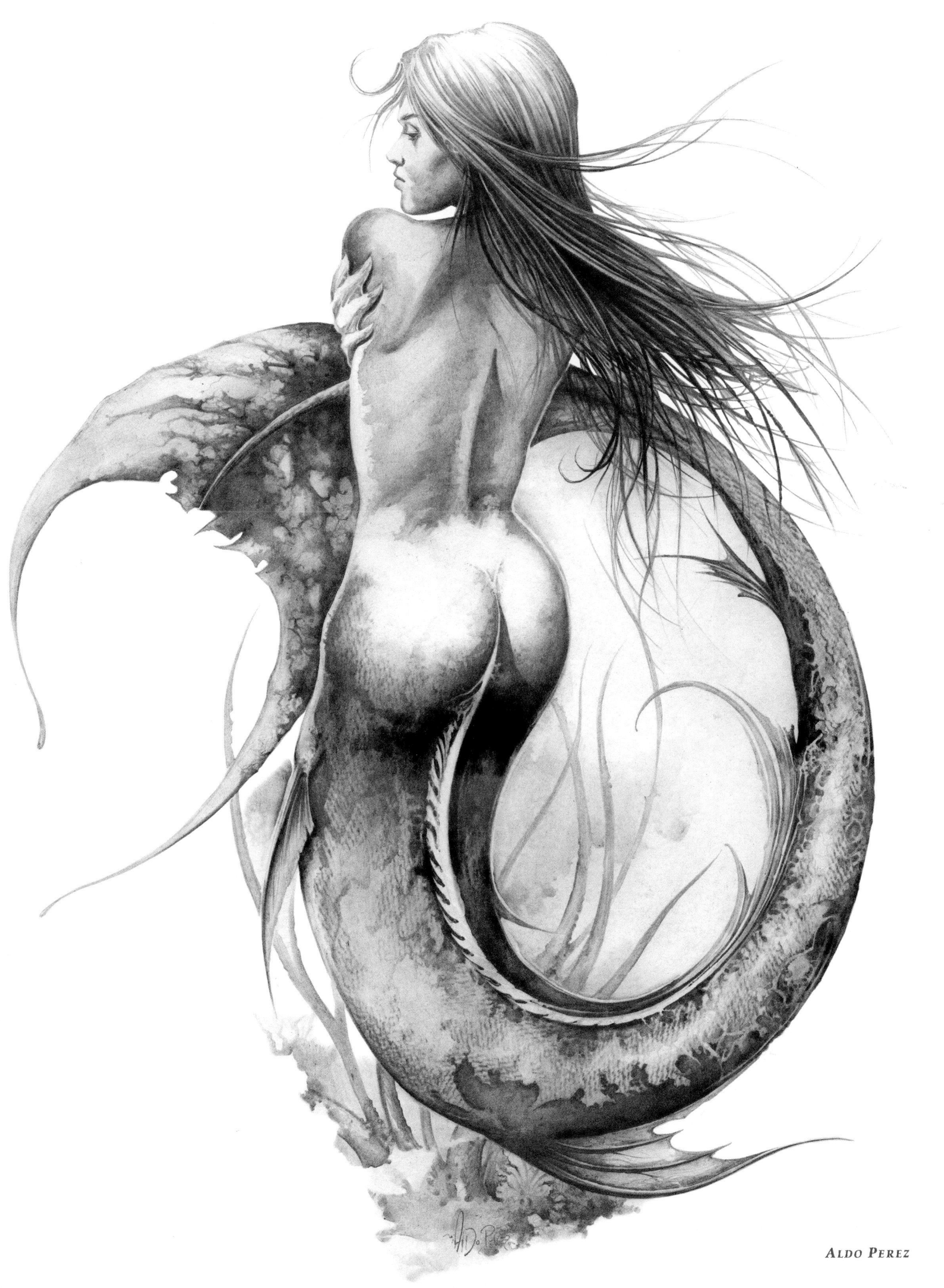

Aldo Perez

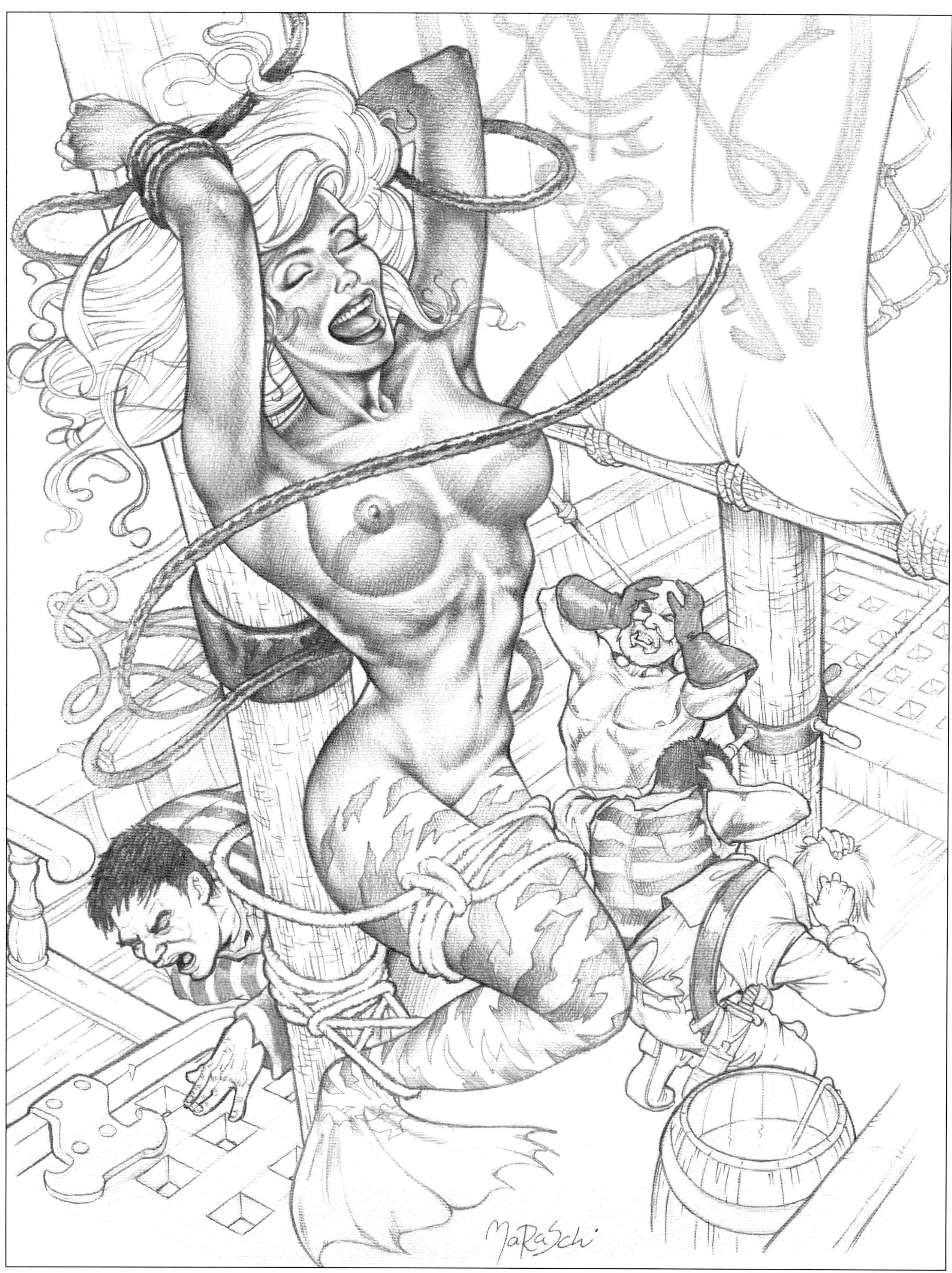

ANIBAL MARASCHI

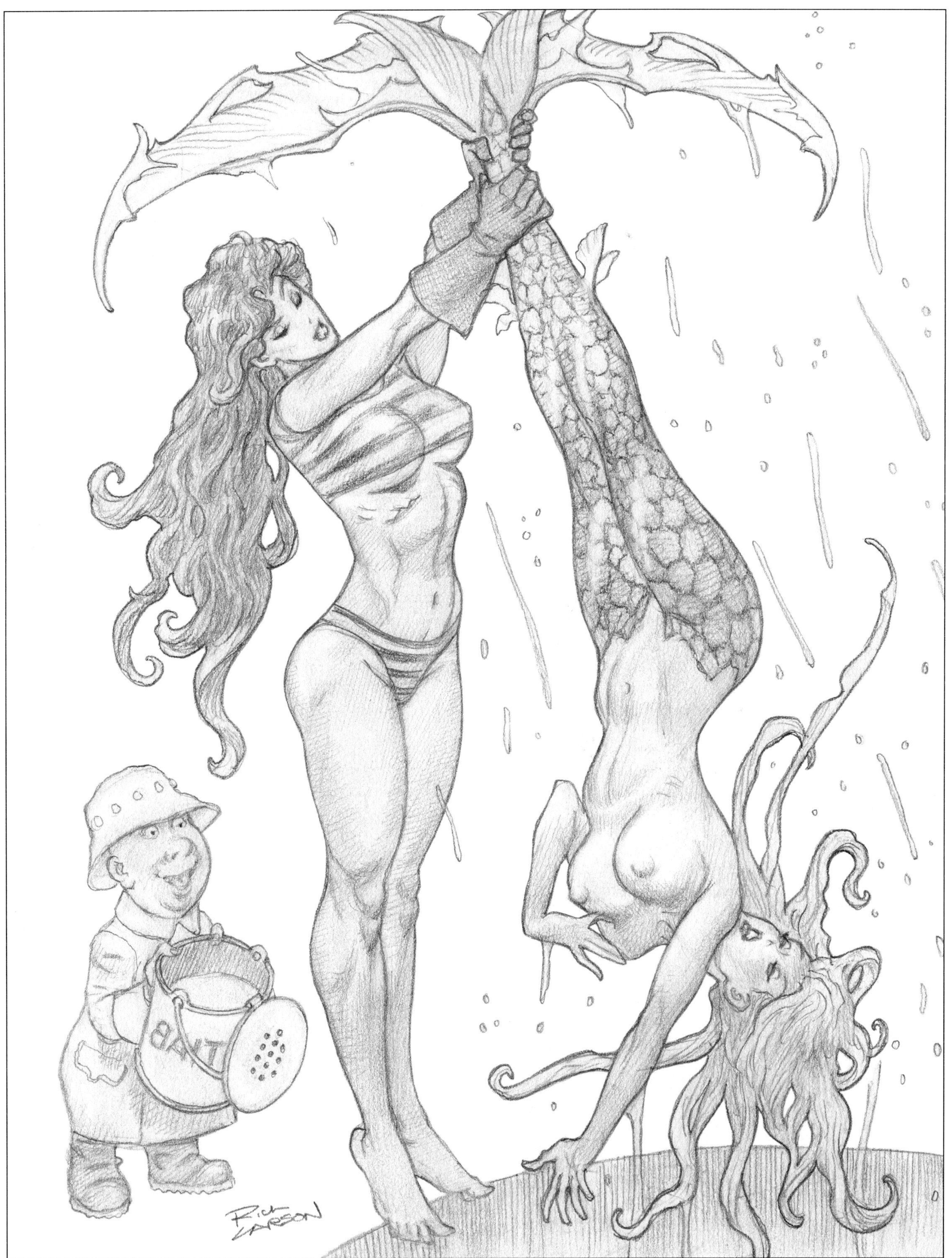

RICH LARSON

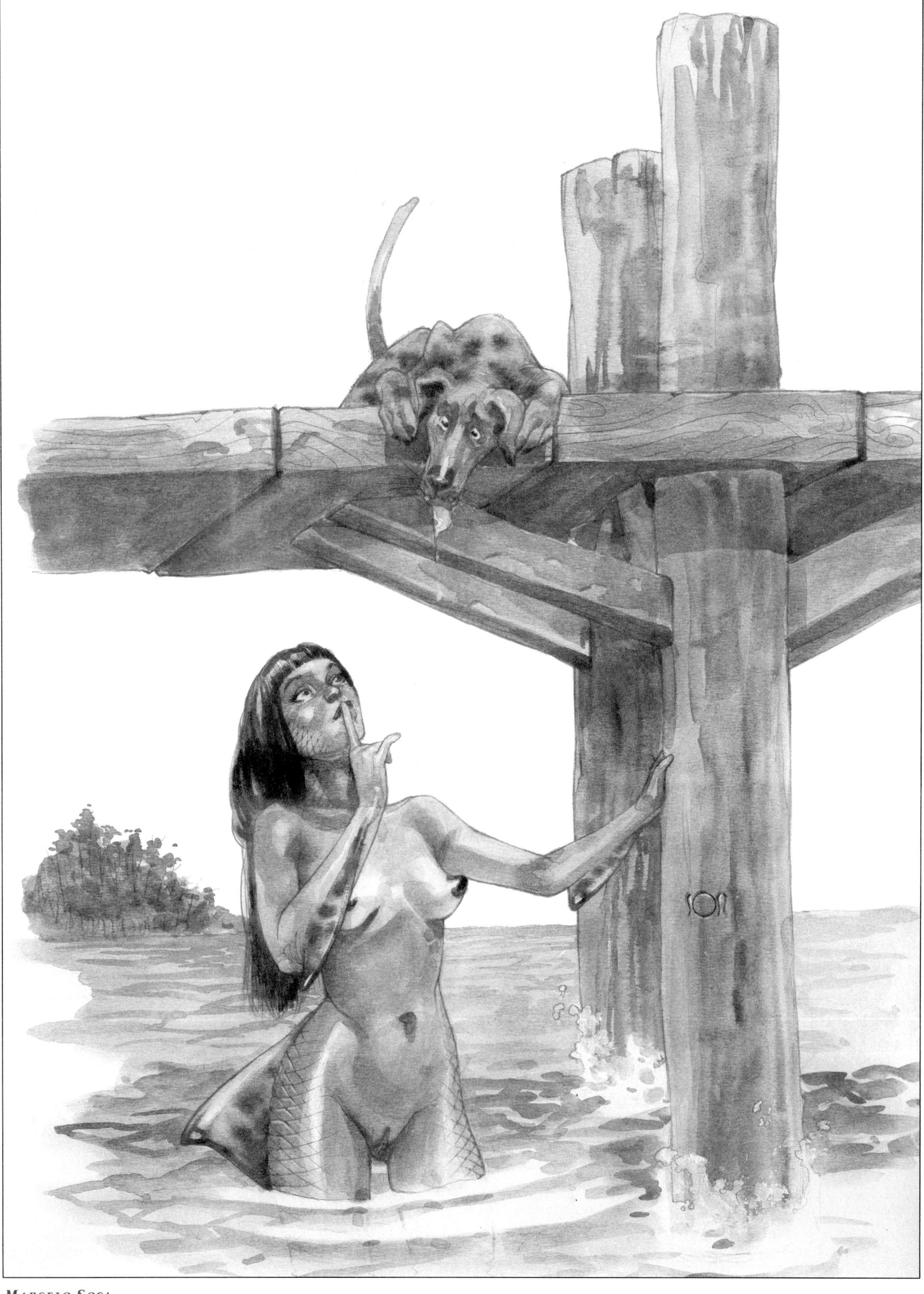

Marcelo Sosa

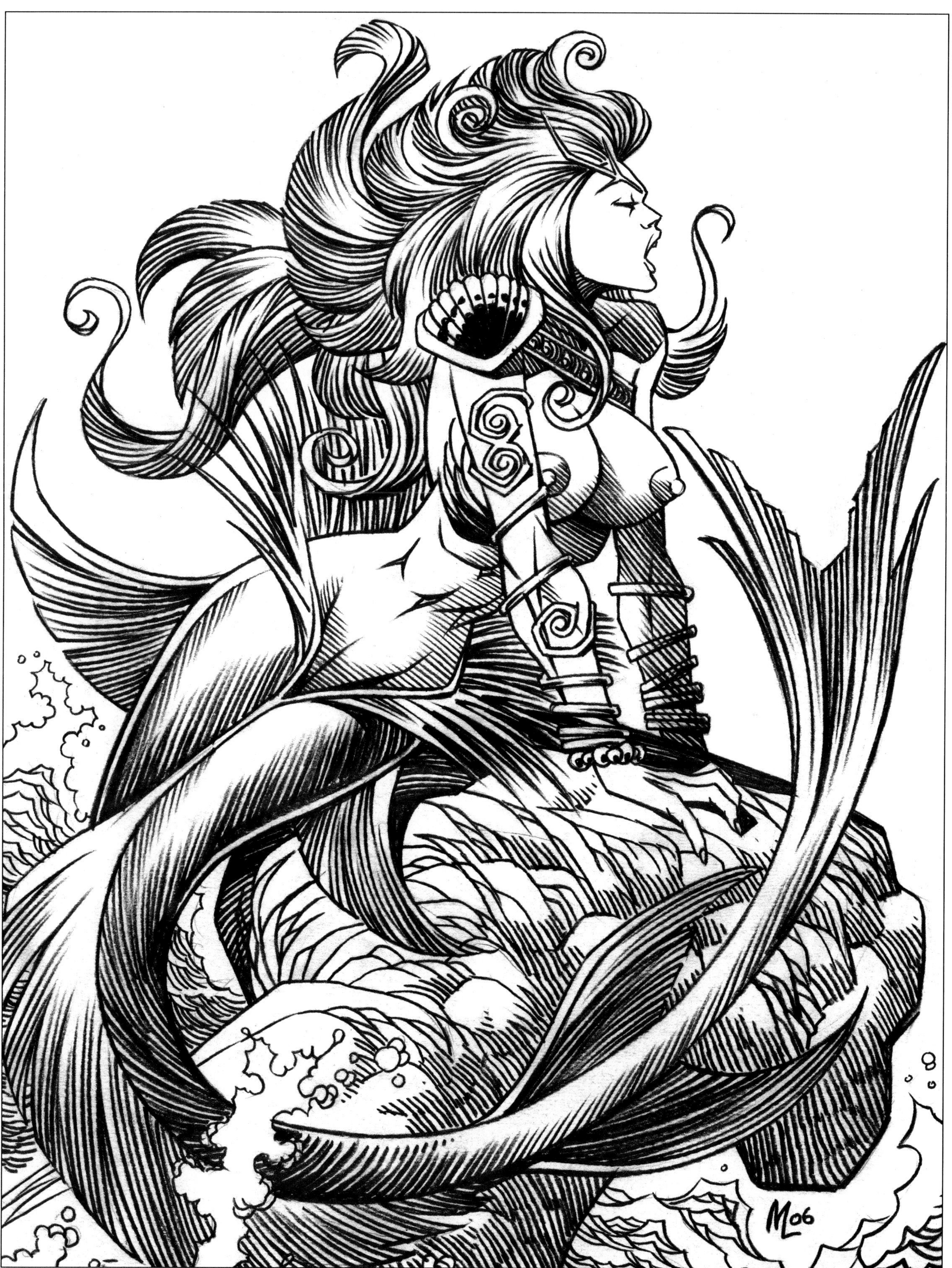

RUBEN MERIGGI

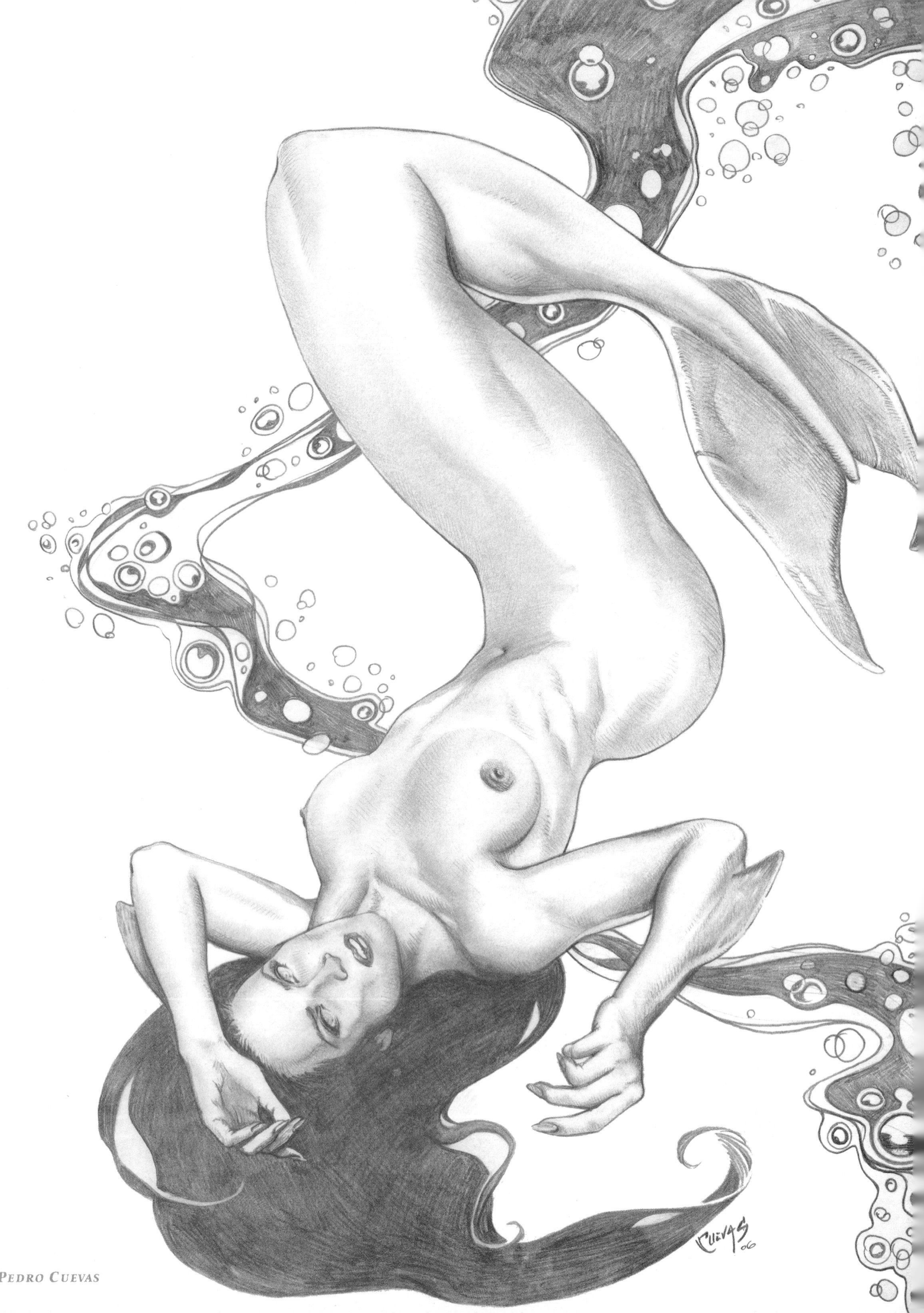

PEDRO CUEVAS

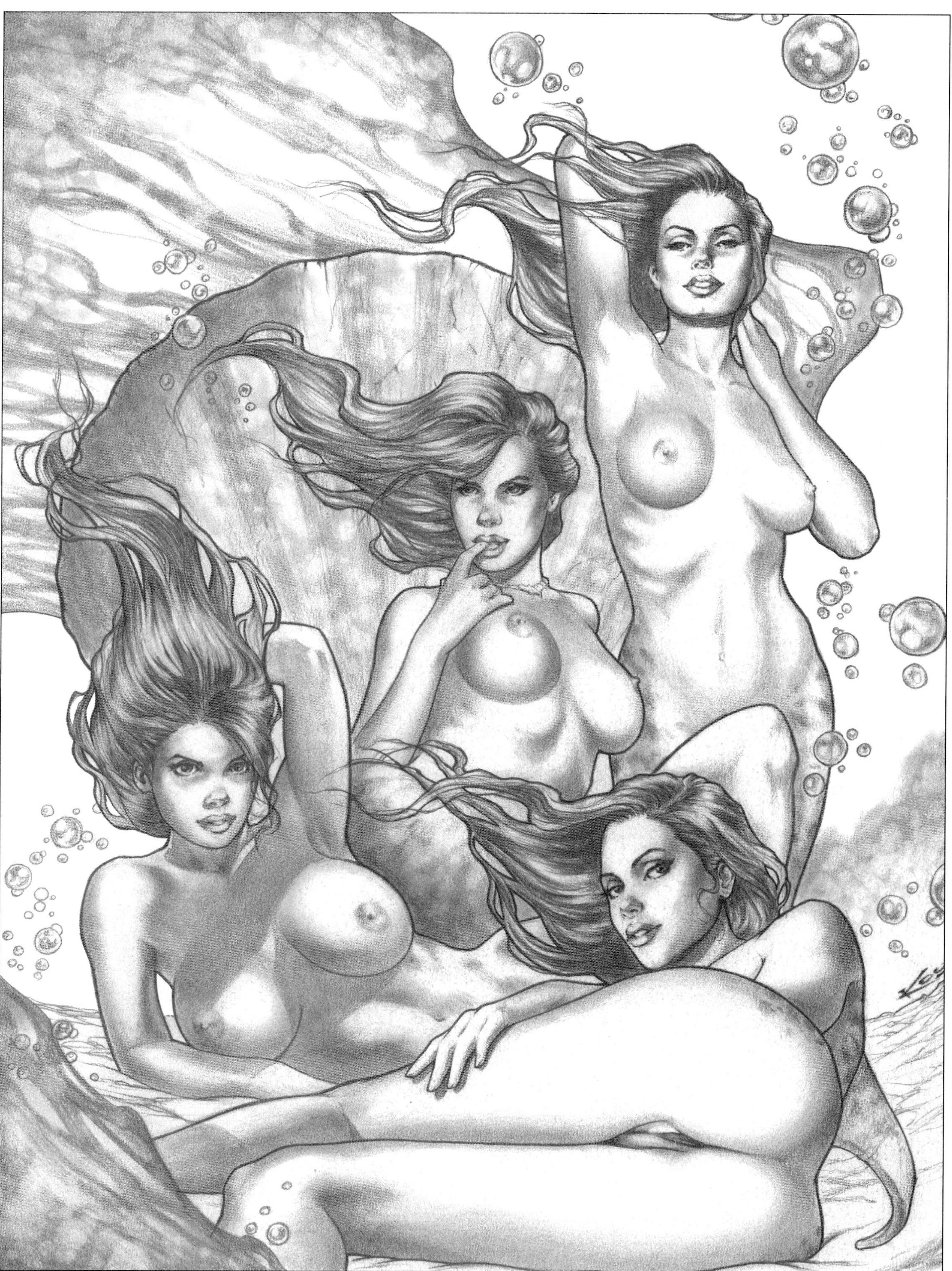

Pablo Kousovitis

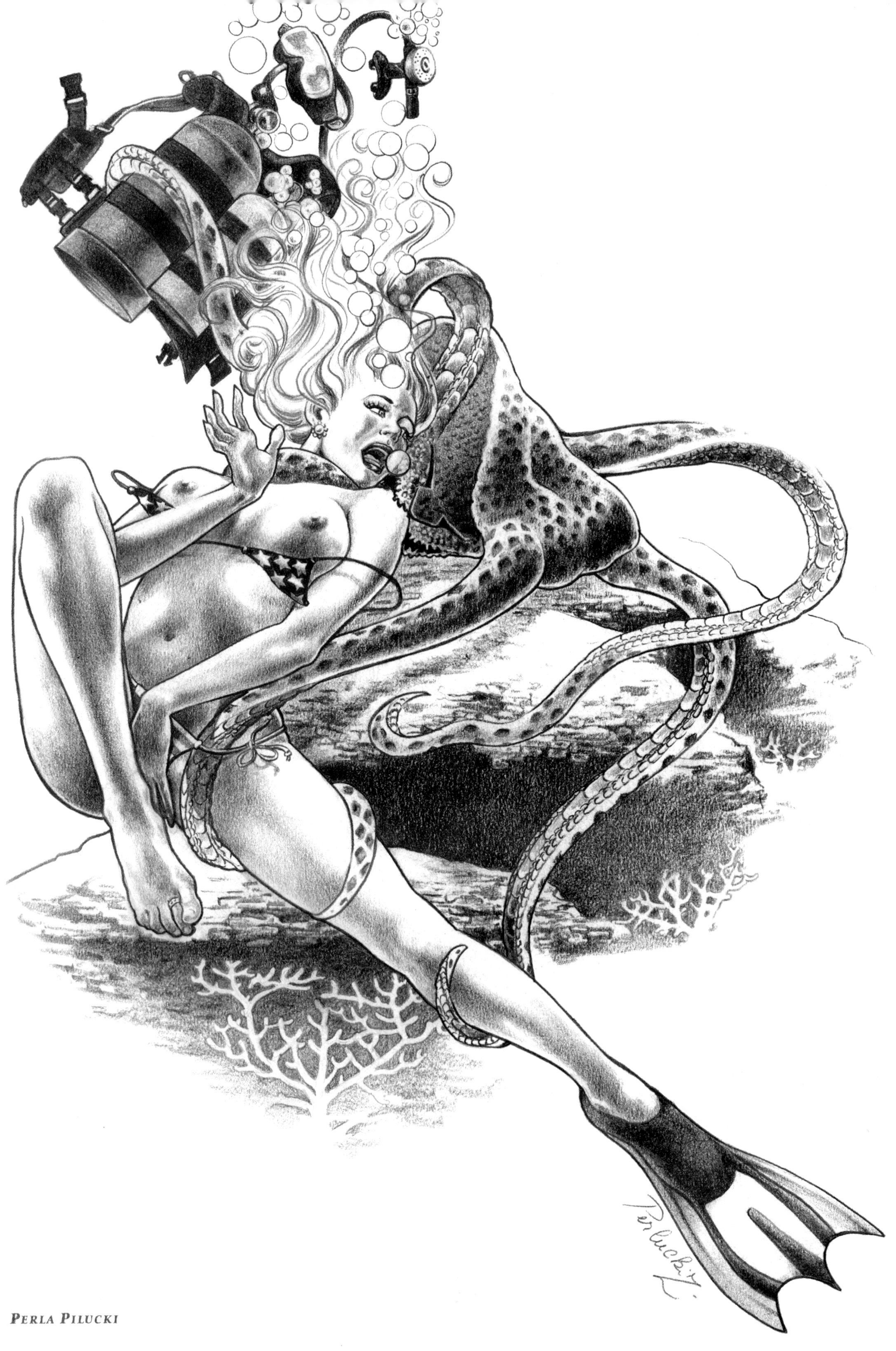

Perla Pilucki

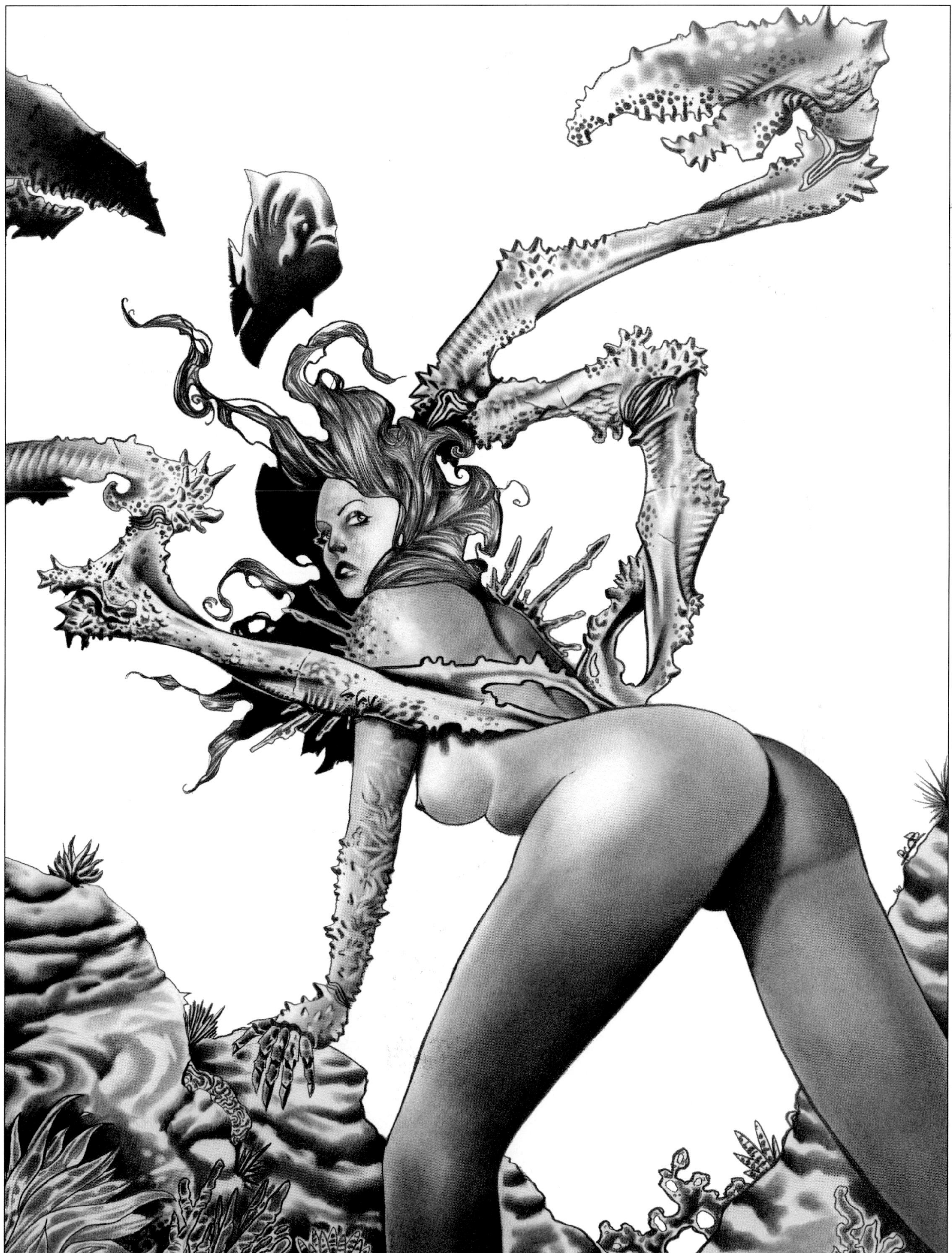

Luis Buci

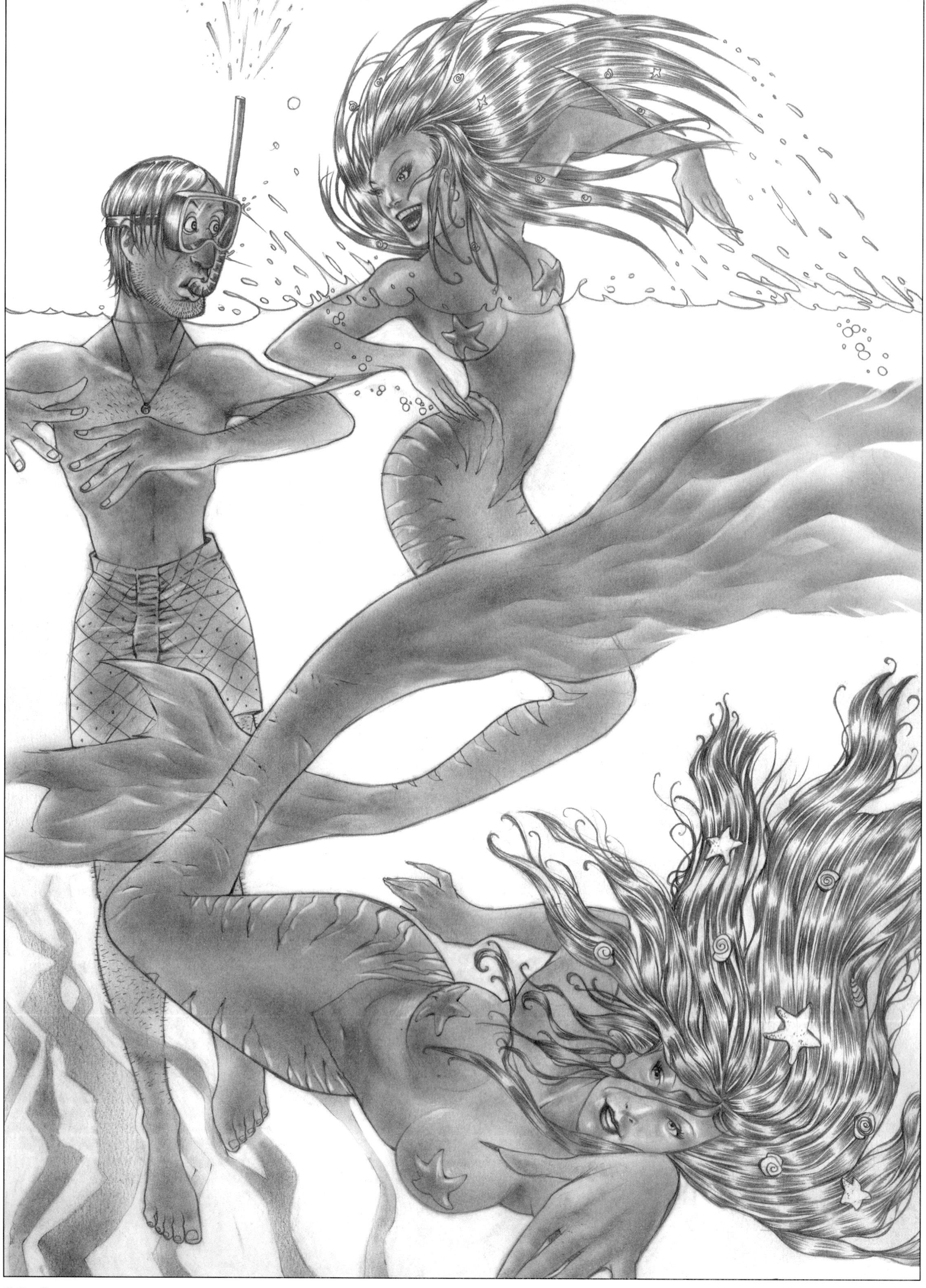

J.L. Czerniawski

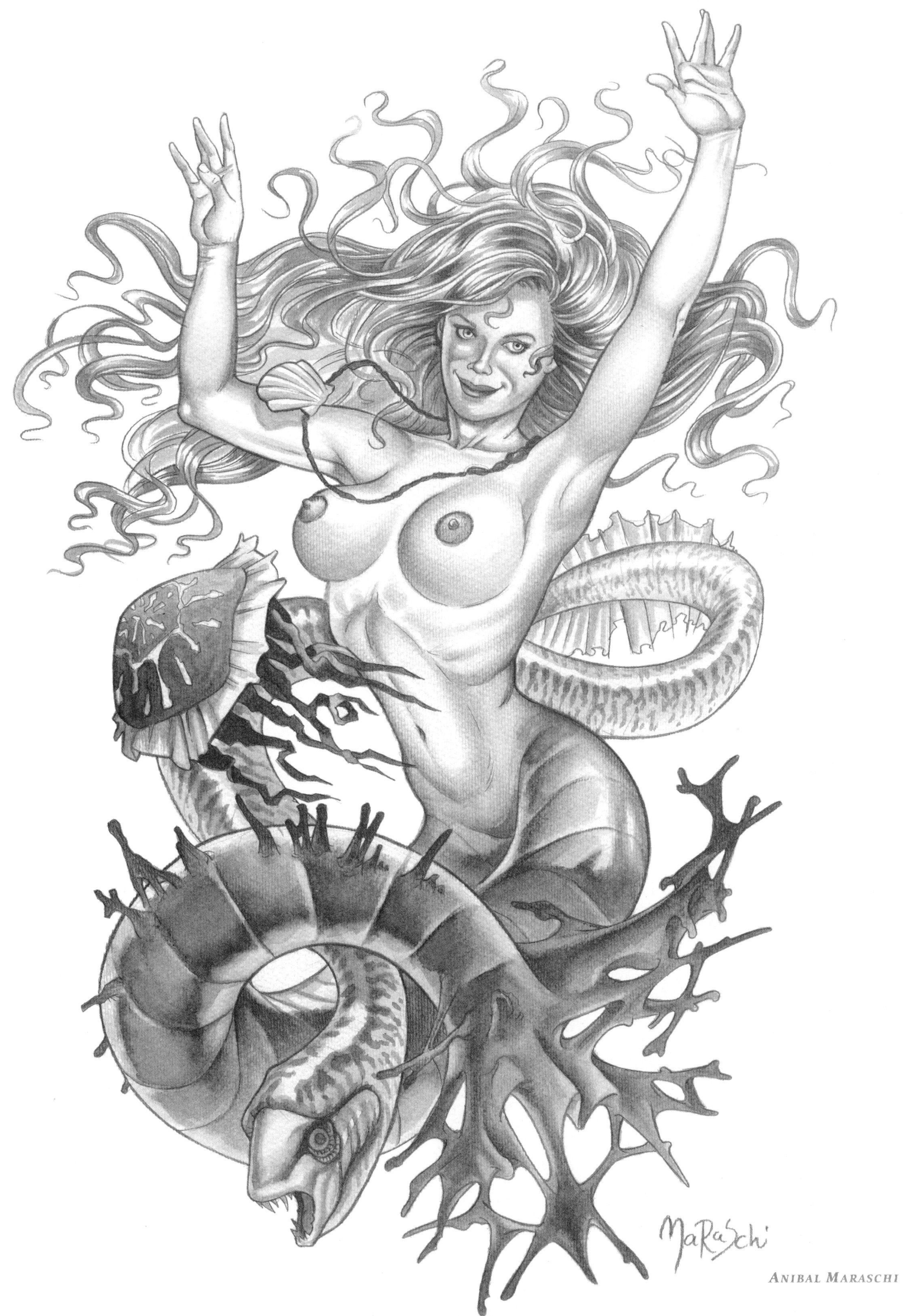

Anibal Maraschi

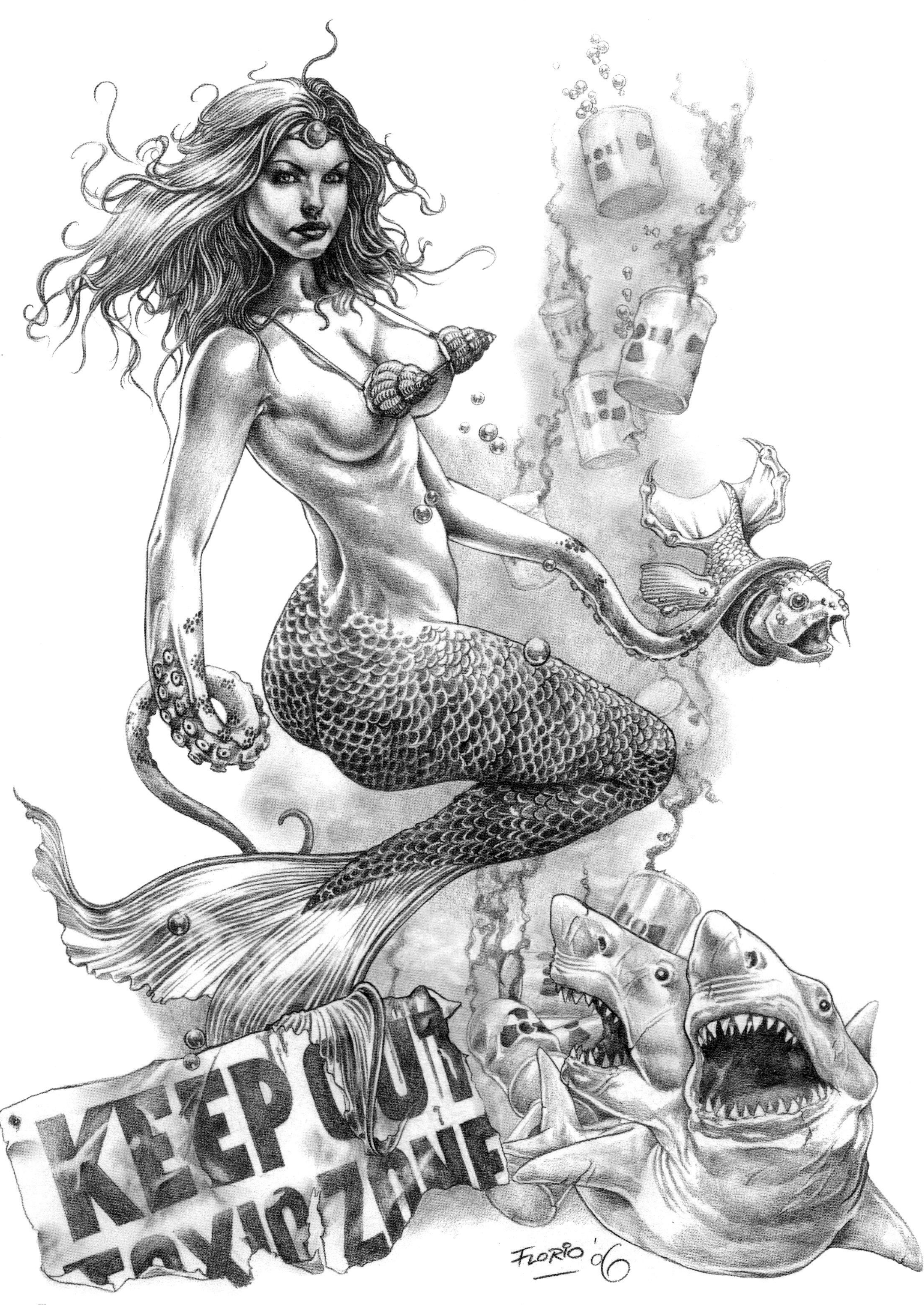

Diego Florio

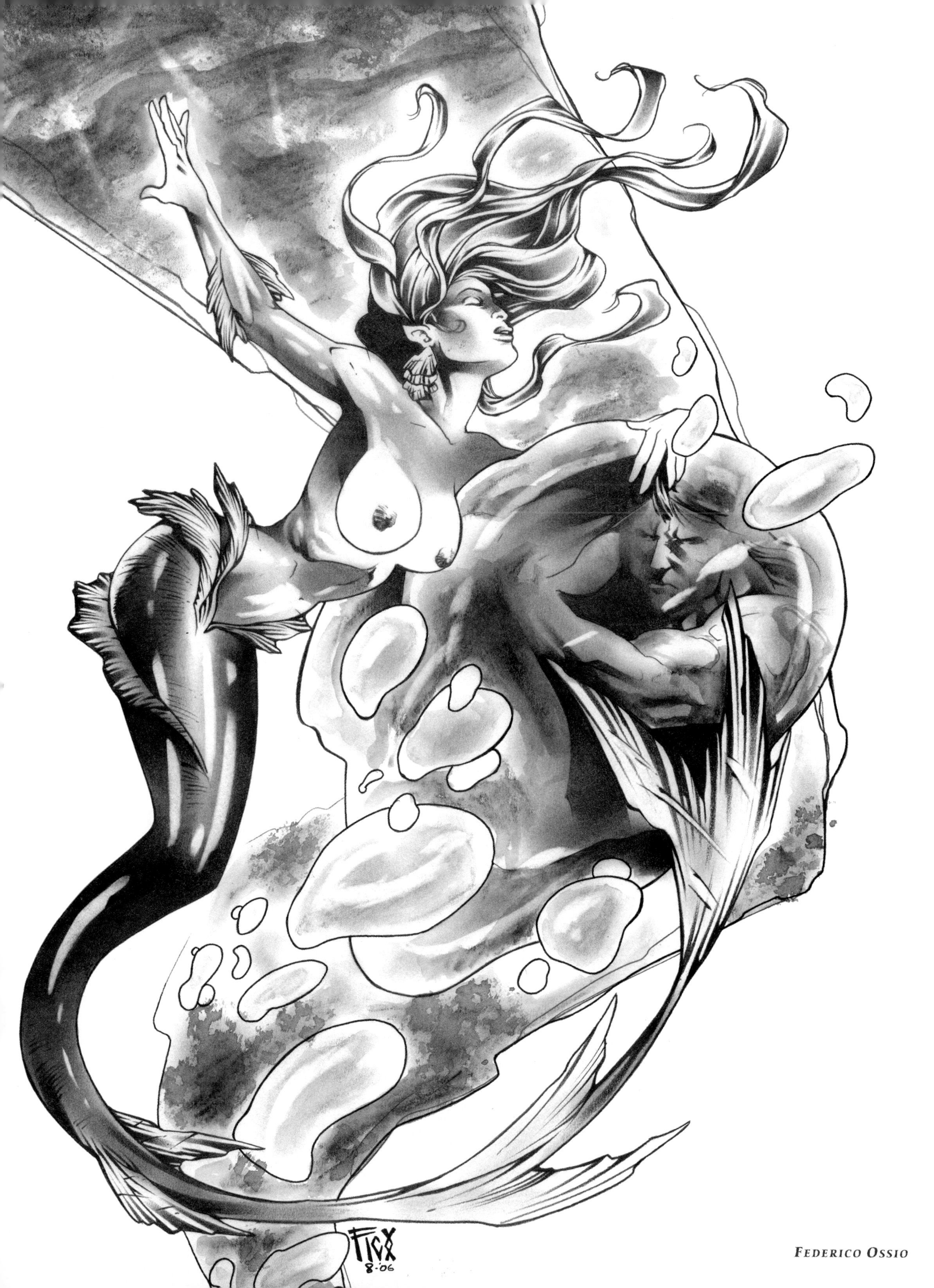

Federico Ossio

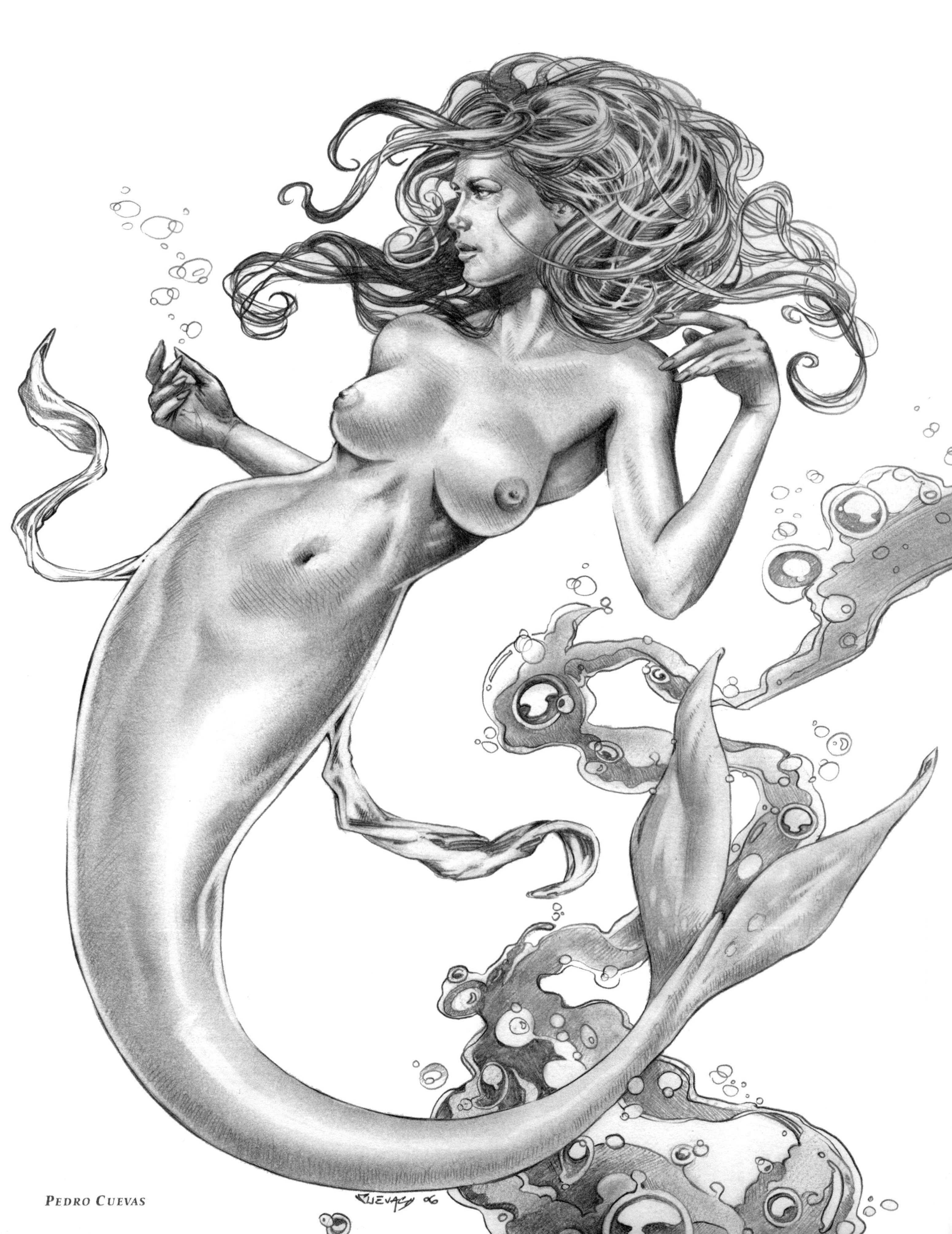

Pedro Cuevas

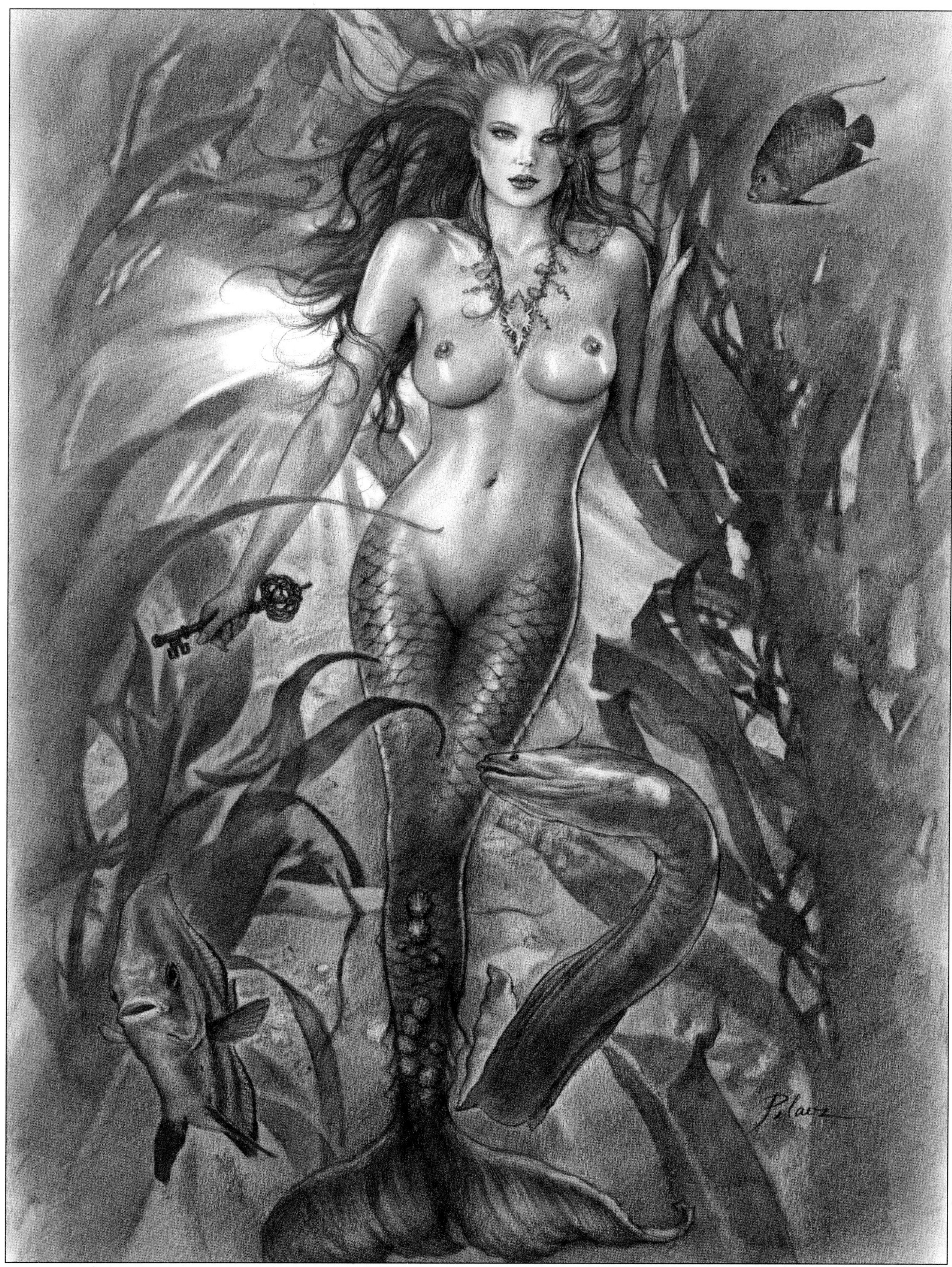

PELAEZ

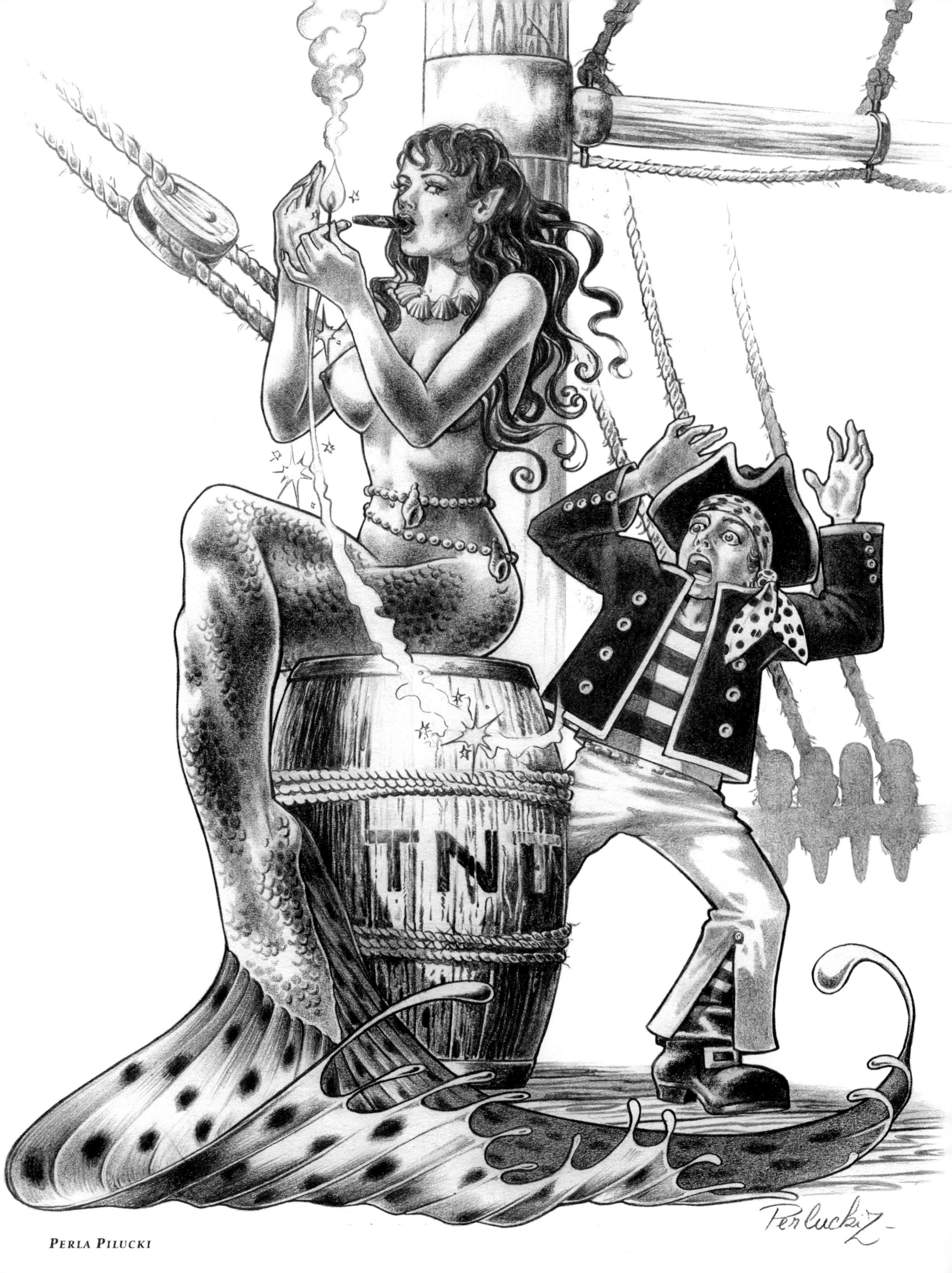

Perla Pilucki

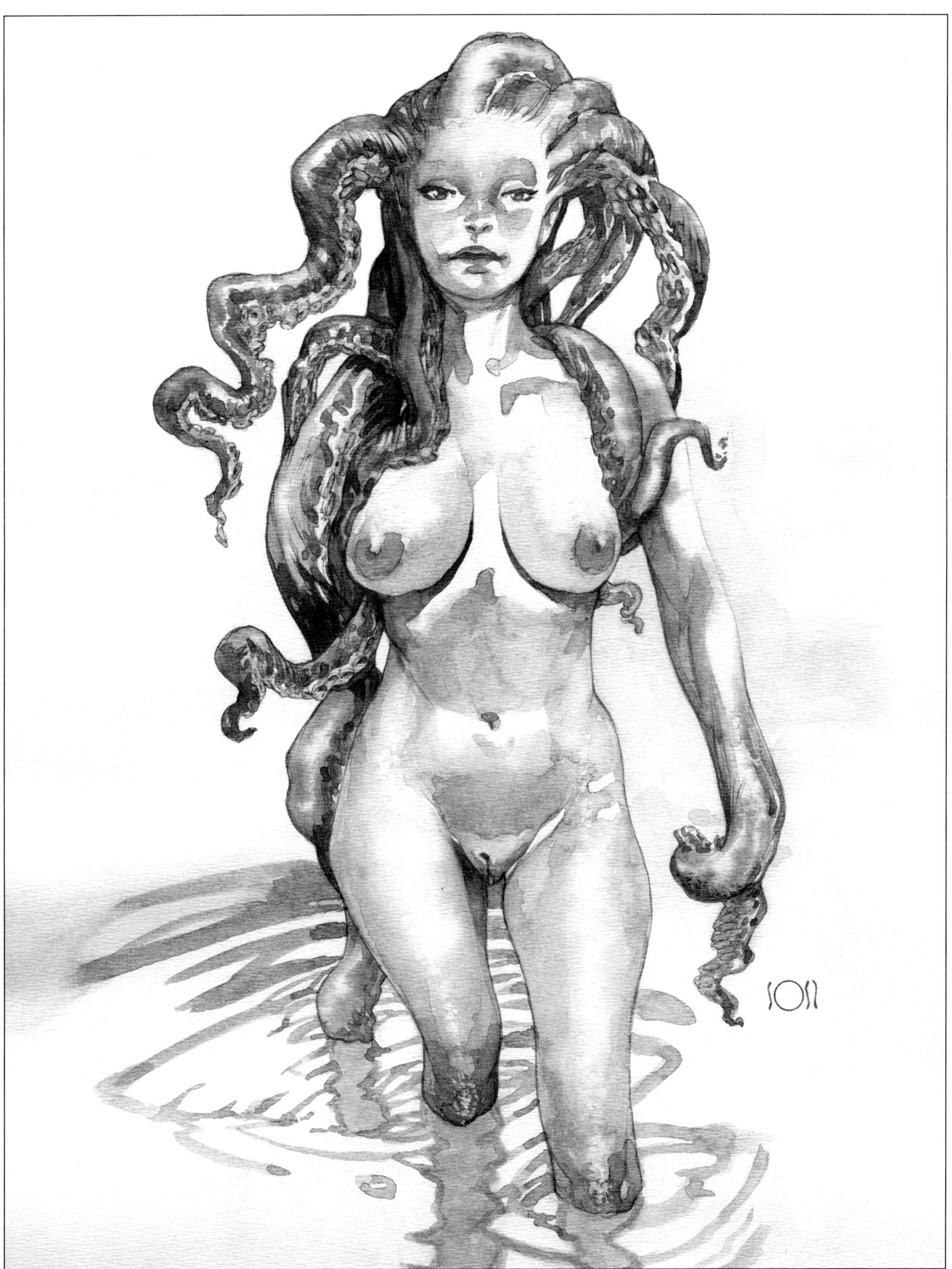

Marcelo Sosa

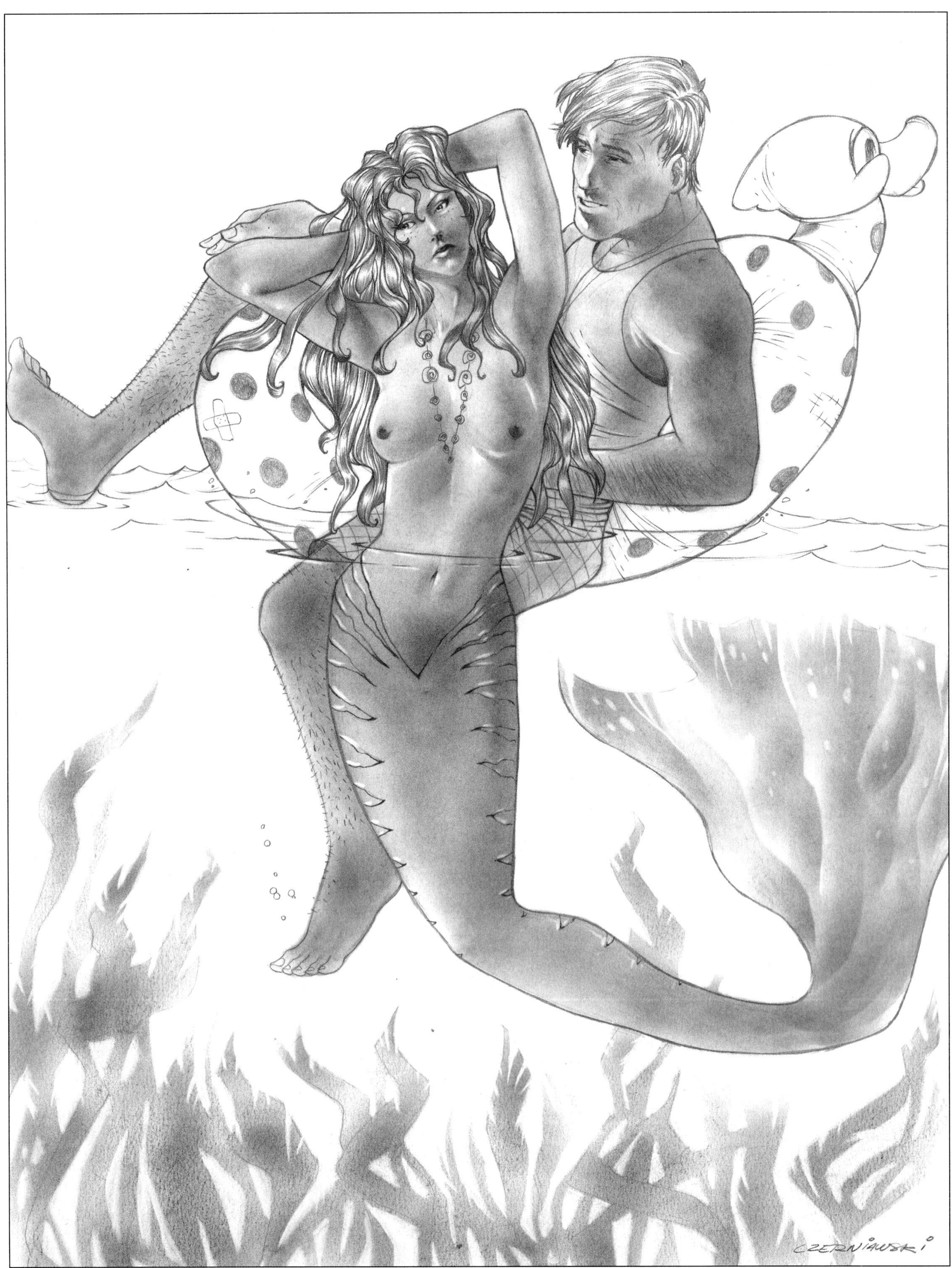

J.L. Czerniawski

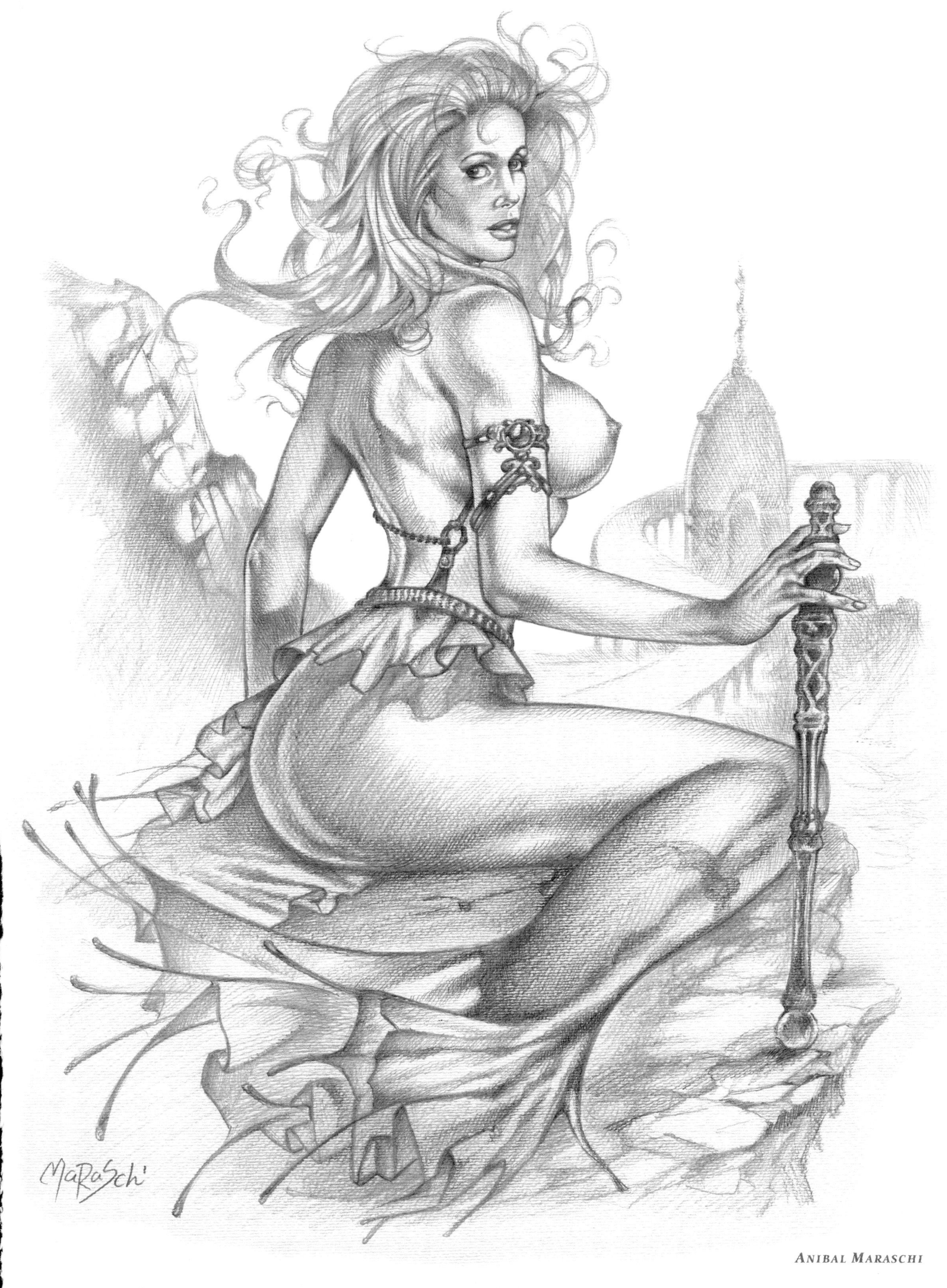

ANIBAL MARASCHI

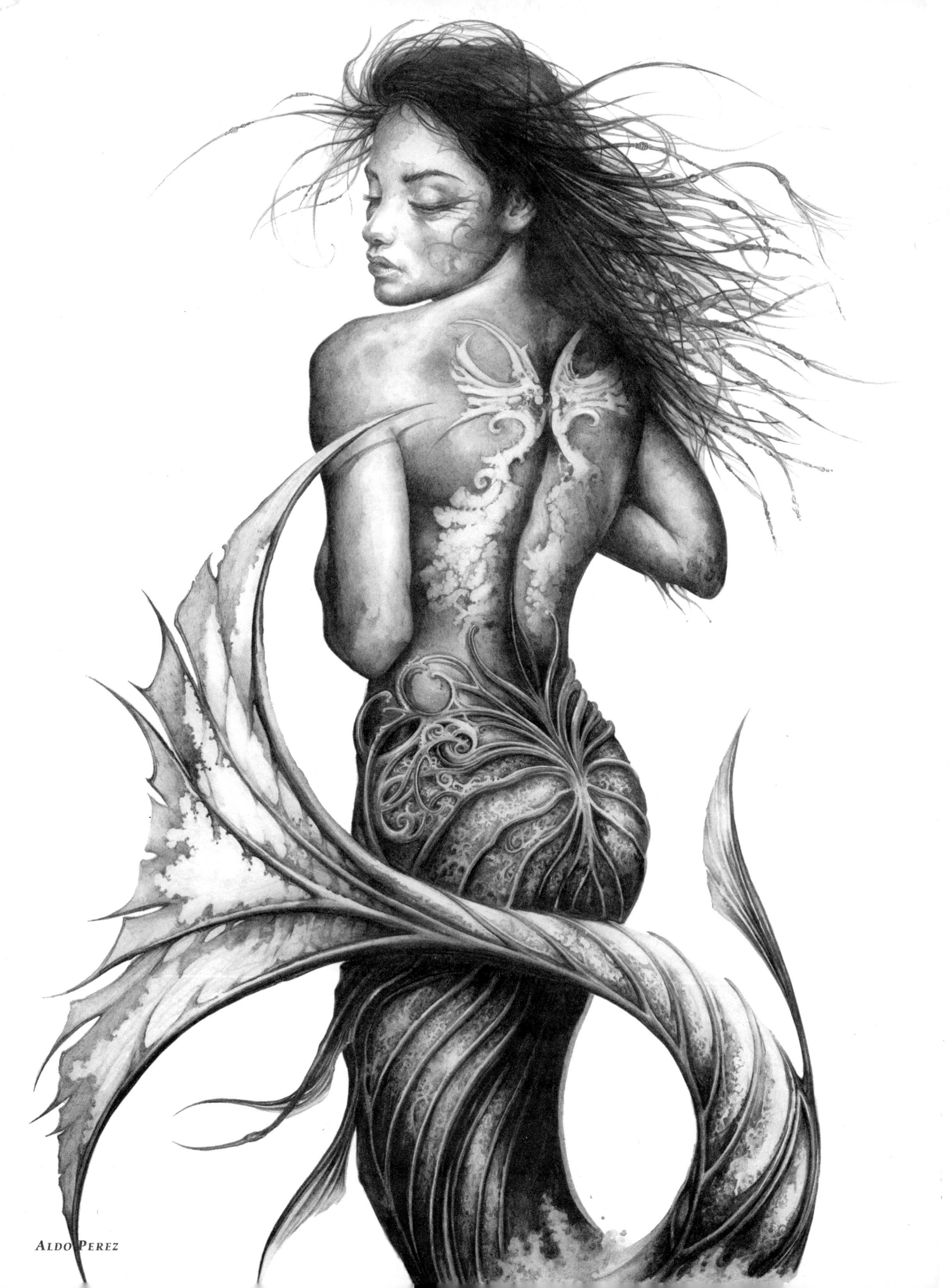
ALDO PEREZ